# HANGED
## FOR A SHEEP
## CRIME IN BYGONE SUSSEX

Dick Richardson

COUNTRY BOOKS

Published by Country Books
Courtyard Cottage, Little Longstone, Bakewell, Derbyshire DE45 1NN
Tel/Fax: 01629 640670
e-mail: dickrichardson@country-books.co.uk

ISBN 1 898941 85 8

*A catalogue of titles published by Country Books and Ashridge Press
is available upon request.*

Printed and bound by: Antony Rowe Ltd.

# INTRODUCTION

This book surveys crime and the treatment of criminals in bygone Sussex, illustrated with extracts from late 18th century copies of the Sussex Weekly Advertiser, the county's first weekly newspaper..

"You may as well be hanged for a sheep as a lamb."

The saying dates back to the days when sheeep-stealing was punishable by death. For stealing a lamb you would be "hanged by the neck until you were dead." The same punishment was meted out for stealing a sheep, so you ran no greater risk for stealing the more valuable article. (This law was repealed in 1828.) Of course, there were other crimes besides sheep-stealing, and more than 200 carried the death penalty or transportation.

Confidence tricksters abounded, even before the days of 'time-share' holidays and 'show-homes' for double-glazing salesmen.

Penalties for 'petty' crimes seem extremely harsh by today's standards, though it must be remembered that there was little or no guidance on sentencing. Prevention of crime and the apprehension of criminals was very much a voluntary effort – paid officials were rare. The government selected wealthy landowners and gave them the title Justice of the Peace. Four times a year, most JP's met for the Quarter Sessions where more serious crimes were tried. For some crimes, the accused was held in custody to await trial by the judges of the Assize Court, on their annual circuit of the country.

But the men in the front line were the parish constables. Untrained volunteers, they were responsible for the arrest of criminals and searching for stolen goods. Many places in the county instituted their own societies, offering a reward for the capture of felons.

Public whippings were commonplace and served as a warning to the populace. The sentence of "until the back be bloody" usually meant 150 lashes plus! The stocks and pillory were still in use as they made criminals known to the public. Prisons were very small, and apart from Houses of Correction, were not regarded as punishment in themselves. The latter held beggars, rogues and vagabonds who were made to work to earn their keep – to 'reform their character'. The keeper had to report on work undertaken and estimate the value, which supposedly paid for the inmates food, clothing and upkeep of the House!

Transportation to America ceased in 1775 on the outbreak of the War of Independence, and prisoners were not shipped to Botany Bay until 1787. In the interim, prisoners were held on prison hulks (unseaworthy men-of-war) in the Thames estuary.

With more than 90 miles of coastline, and the proximity of France and Holland, there has always been problems with smuggling. For the last millennium we were smuggling out wool and sheep and bringing in alcohol, lace, tea, tobacco, etc. In 1794 an Act of Parliament was passed allowing Revenue Officers to seek military assistance – for a share of the profits. This was not popular!

The report of 21st April 1788, I suspect is a piece of 'journalistic licence'. Informers against smugglers were normally killed, but this report seems to indicate that they were quite jolly people.

Ignoring smuggling, Sussex crime was probably no worse than many inland counties, though the following extract from the *Tourist's Guide to the County of Sussex* by George F Chambers, published in 1891, shows that suspicion remained, 100 years after the extracts in this book.

*"The most serious drawback to Seaford is the civility on the part of the real 'natives.' This last-named characteristic is reputed to be due to the lawless wrecking spirit which survives to the present day, derived from former generations of inhabitants, notorious wreckers and smugglers, plus the corruption of morals induced by men's votes having been worth £1000. There is still discernible among the people of Seaford a mixture of cringing servility and vulgar bullying..."*

One suspects that Seaford inhabitants were waiting the return of George Chambers with a lynch mob!

# CONFIDENCE TRICKSTERS

## September 12TH 1791
A CAUTION. A Man apparently about fifty years of age has within the last fortnight, endeavoured to impose on several tradesmen and others, in the neighbourhood of Cuckfield and Horsham.

## June 18TH 1792
To the many knaveties practised on and by parish officers the following anecdote affords a pleasing contrast: One Mitchell, a parishioner of West Chiltington, in this county, having incurred debts which he was unable to pay, absconded about two years ago, and left his family chargeable to the parish; but the present overseers have lately received a letter from him, expressive of his concern for what necessity had compelled him to do, and generously tending ample compensation for the maintenance of children during his absence.

Different was the conduct of a fellow of Shipley parish, which he left burdened with a mistress and child, and revisited not till after an absence of more than 20 years. His appearance then bespoke feebleness and beggary, but the parish failed not to remind her prodigal son of his former gallantry. Before the Justice he piteously pleaded poverty, and tendered three guineas as the whole gleaning of an unsuccessful life. The officials, who believed his tale, unfeelingly seized the wretched pittance, and releasing him from any further claim became the dupes of his artifice, and their own rapaciousness. For the knave, thus secured by a legal acquittance, changed his tone and garb; purchased houses in the parish, and laughed at its petty governors.

## July 16TH 1792
A shopkeeper at Rushlake Green has lately been tricked out of goods to the amount of near £10; and a person at Hellingly, out of £3 in cash, by a gang of swindlers. To the latter one of them personated a Swedish captain of whom another (his accomplice) could make a very advantageous purchase of smuggled 1ace, if he had money enough, and under that pretext prevailed on his credulous friend to

lend him the sum above mentioned.

A personal description of such vagabond imposters would now be of little use; nor is there much pity due to the avaricious credulity of those that are taken in by such hackneyed deceptions.

### July 29TH 1793

A few days since a genteel well-dressed young man with a lady attended by a black servant, arrived at the Norfolk Arms, Arundel, where he soon found means so far to ingratiate himself with a gentleman of that town, so as to procure the loan of £250, with which he shortly after decamped, and has not since been heard of. He assumed the title of *Earl of Rutlandshire*.

### August 12TH 1793

The public are cautioned against a female impostor who by her various artifices, but too often successfully imposes upon the unwary, Her first business is to learn the connections of the persons she means to impose upon, after which she finds but little difficulty in insinuating herself into favour, by means of a pretended recommendation from them. She is a tall woman of middle age, pitted with the small pox, and for the most part wears a black bombazine gown.

### April 28TH 1794

On Saturday se'nnight two women, who had arrived at Brighton the preceding evening in a carrier's waggon, took a very genteel lodging house belonging to a Mr Bonne, adjoining Mrs Hamilton, on the Steine, at that place, at the rent of three guineas and a half per week; which they at first pretended was for a family with whom they lived as servants. In this capacity they had given orders for several articles necessary for house keeping; but some part of their conduct having been suspected as not being altogether consonant with the character they had assumed, they threw off the servile appellation of dependents, and declared themselves ladies of small fortune who had travelled from Bath (their native place). The proprietor of the house, however, not better satisfied with his lodgers in their new character, than in their former one, placed a guard at the door to save the ladies the trouble of removing any part of his property.

On Thursday and Friday the blockaded ladies were necessitated to appear at the windows of their castle, as they termed it, to answer the clamour of near a hundred Poissardes, and other persons who had assembled about the door demanding that they would come forth and decamp with as little baggage as they possessed when they entered, namely, the clothes which were upon their backs.

On Saturday last the above ladies were reduced to the necessity of a capitulation. They offered to quit provided a Post Chaise should be hired and paid for by the Landlord to convey them to this place; that they should be protected from the vengeance of the fish women who had hugely threatened them; and to have the week's rent remitted them; all which being acceded to by the landlord, they set off, and arrived here [Lewes] about 3 o'clock in the afternoon; but their fame having alighted before them, they could get no admittance into any house whatever, and they departed hence on foot the same afternoon.

January 5TH 1795

Last Thursday a young woman of genteel appearance visited this town [Lewes] and by virtue of a certificate (which appeared to be authenticated by the signatures of two Magistrates of Bridgwater) aided by her innocent appearance and artless demeanour, obtained money from many charitable persons.

The certificate represented her as the widow of Thomas Lamb, a native of Rye, in this county, and captain of the *Hope*, which had been sunk in an engagement with a French ship. The above instrument also stated that the Captain, his wife, crew and passengers had been rescued from the *Hope* before she sunk by a vessel belonging to Bridgwater, which had carried them into that port, where the captain having received a wound from a musket shot in the engagement, died three days after he had landed.

A circumstance, however, on Saturday occurred that leads us to suspect the whole is an imposition, but as no positive proof of it yet has arrived, we for the present dismiss the subject with observing it is no wonder that Miss P — should have been so much deceived by this American lady, when it is generally allowed that no one could better have played the character she personated, namely the Child of Misfortune.

### January 13<sup>TH</sup> 1795

The lady to whom we alluded in our issue as the pretended widow of one Captain Thomas Lamb has now confirmed the suspicions we entertained of her by absconding to avoid the consequences that might have followed the impositions which she had practised, in different places on the public. This female trickster to prevent any other restraint being laid upon her, was prevailed on to deposit ten guineas with the Clerk of the Justice before whom she underwent an examination as a sort of security for her stay here, until inquiry could be made concerning her well-told narrative; but conscious of her guilt, she thought it prudent to forfeit her security and decamp before any information to affect her could be received. She is a decent looking young woman, with dark eyes, is low of stature, and was dressed in a black riding habit with a beaver hat of the same colour. She was equally successful in her collections at Arundel and Brighton as at this place (Lewes) where she would not have been detected but from its being understood that no such person as she pretended to be the widow of had ever existed.

### July 13<sup>TH</sup> 1795

The Magnetical Doctor who lately held forth here from his coach in recommendation of his Vermifugis pulvis of Anti-Vermatical worm-conquering powder, exhibited to the gaping multitude, a curious collection of worms, one of which he said, measured the length of *two hundred and twenty yeards*! It was an unfortunate circumstance for those anthropagous vermin that the doctor's neck should have evaded the hempen belt in America where he says he was tried for his attachment to Royalty, with two others that were hanged, and whose fate he declared he escaped by dint of money only, with which he bribed "the Judge, Jury and all."

# DUELS

## February 6<sup>TH</sup> 1792

Last Thursday morning a butcher and a shopkeeper of Burwash, in this county, went into a field near Lewes with pistols, to decide a quarrel of long standing between them. The lusty knight of the cleaver, having made it a practice to insult his antagonist, who is a very little man; the great disparity between them in size rendered this the only eligible alternative for the latter. The butcher took care to inform his wife of the intended meeting in hopes she would give the Constables timely notice thereof. But the good woman not having felt so deeply interested in his fate as he expected, to make sure, he sent to the Constable himself, and then marched reluctantly to the field; where the little spirited shopkeeper was parading with a considerable reserve of ammunition, lest his first shot should not take effect. Now the affrightened butcher proceeded slowly to charge his pistols, alternately looking towards the town and his impatient adversary. This man of blood, all pale and trembling, at last began to despair of any friendly interference, when the Constable very seasonably appeared, and forbade the duel, to his great joy, and the disappointment of the spectators.

## May 4<sup>TH</sup> 1795

A few mornings ago a duel was fought near Preston hedges, between an artillery officer at Brighton and another belonging to the Lancashire Fencibles quartered there. They discharged a brace of pistols each, but neither took effect, when the seconds interfered, and through their mediation the champions quitted the field of honour, quite cool, and apparently in perfect friendship.

## March 31<sup>ST</sup> 1800

T. Harben, Esq; the Bailiff of Seaford. having between eleven and twelve o'clock on last Thursday night, received information that Lieutenant T and J. O—c, Esq; were to meet at six the next morning on the beach, near the Signal post, for the purpose of fighting a duel, ordered the Constable to take the parties immediately into custody, who in consequence caused Mr. O. to be called from his bed, and made a prisoner of him; but the Lieutenant, to elude his search, concealed himself the whole night in a bathing machine, and in the morning, attended with his second at the time and place appointed, where he waited two hours for the arrival of his antagonist, and then retired to his apartment in the barrack, where he was also taken into custody. They were, however, soon after liberated, on finding two sureties, who entered into recognizances of £150 each, for their keeping the peace towards each other in future.

The challenge, we understand, arose from a dispute between the parties, touching the priority of claim to certain young lady in the neighbourhood.


## FOOTPADS AND HIGHWAYMEN

### May 16TH 1774

On Tuesday night last, between ten and eleven o'clock as one of the boys belonging to the Post Office in this town [Lewes] was returning from Eastbourne (where he had been on some particular occasion) a man suddenly leaped from a hedge and endeavoured to seize his horse's bridle, at the same time crying out "stand and deliver," but the horse starting at the sudden motion of the man, jumped off the causeway when the boy embraced the opportunity, clapped spurs to his horse and rode by him, whereupon the man instantly discharged a pistol the ball from which the boy positively asserts came whistling by his ear. He received no other injury than being terribly frightened.


### September 26TH 1774

On Tuesday evening last as Lady Harcourt accompanied by some other ladies, was going to her carriage to the Ball at Tunbridge Wells, it was stopped near Speldhurst Common by a single highwayman, who after robbing the ladies of near £20 in money, demanded their jewels; but at that instant the driver, who had before quitted his horse and crept slyly along the pole on the carriage, seized the highwayman by the arm, who plunging violently, disengaged himself, and after snapping his pistol at the driver, which fortunately only flashed in the pan, got clean off.

The villain in his flight dropped his pistol, and 'tis thought would have been secured had the footman exerted himself equally with his fellow servant; but he never once offered his assistance.

### December 11<sup>TH</sup> 1775

On Sunday night, as one of the boys belonging to the Post Office, Lewes, was returning with the mail from Steyning he was attacked between that place and Shoreham, on the Downs near Erringham, by a single footpad, who presented a pistol to his breast, and took from him three shillings and the Mail containing the London bags, with letters for Shoreham and Brighthelmstone; also the Haslemere, Petworth, Arundel and Steyning bye bags. The next day, about twelve o'clock the said Mail was found hid in a furze bush, about half-a-mile distant from the spot where the boy said he had been robbed, containing all the above bags, and to all appearance had not been opened.

### October 20<sup>TH</sup> 1777

On Friday evening the 10th instant as Mr Dyer, of Copperas Gap, near Brighthelmstone, was returning from Chichester Fair, he was attacked within about a mile of the City, by a single highwayman, who presented a pistol, and demanded his money, upon which Mr Dyer instantly raised his whip and striking the robber a violent blow across his arm with the butt end of it, occasioned him to drop his pistol, and thereby escaped without being robbed.

### February 17<sup>TH</sup> 1783

On Friday night, the 7th inst., as the Petworth stage waggon was on its return from Portsmouth to that place, one of the drivers was stopt on the road by two soldiers who, with drawn swords, ordered him to stop; but the driver being a resolute man, and unwilling to have his master's waggon robbed in his sight, turned his whip and with the great end of it so belaboured the villains that they made off, before his mate, who was a short distance behind, could get up to his assistance. We hope Mr. Challen has not suffered his servant to go unrewarded for his courage and fidelity.

## 14TH April 1783

Last Wednesday, between four and five o'clock in the afternoon, as Richard Pope, a gentleman's servant, was on his road from Handcross to Beeding, in this county, he was attacked by a single footpad, near the Crab Tree, on St. Leonards Forest, who after knocking him down with a bludgeon, and supposing him to be dead, robbed him of £5 2s in money, and a silver watch and made off across the forest. Two persons have since been taken up on suspicion of committing the said robbery, but as nothing appeared against them to justify their detention they were discharged.

## 22ND December 1783

About a week since one W. Pelley, of Chichester was stopped on the road, at the end of Raw Mare Lane, near the above city, by three footpads, who robbed him of a few shillings, but Pelley having, a small distance behind, passed two men, had the presence of mind to keep the robbers in chat till the men came in sight, to whom he immediately gave the alarm, when two of the villains, named Smith and Hartley, were taken and secured, and the next day committed by W. Mill Leeves Esq., to Horsham Gaol.

## August 21ST 1786

Yesterday se'nnight a little after seven in the evening, a most daring highway robbery was committed, on a turnpike road about a mile and a half on this side of Brighthelmston by a single footpad, who stopped a man and his wife in a one-horse chaise, and clapping a large horse-pistol to the breast of the former, robbed him of two half guineas and his wife of 9/- and then d—d their eyes, and ordered them to drive on as fast as they could. The persons robbed saw a man on the road riding towards them at the time, but were too much alarmed at the pistol to make any hesitation in the delivery of their money. On the man's approach they acquainted him with the circumstances, who immediately pursued and overtook the villain, but knowing him to be well armed, did not attack him till he had called some persons to his assistance when he seized and took the robber, and having properly secured him, carried him back to Brighthelmston, where he was next day examined before Mr Sergeant Kempe, who fully committed him to Horsham Gaol, to take his trial for the offence at our next assizes. When taken, he had found upon him two large pistols, loaded with slugs four fingers high, which, with a number of slugs that were loose in his waistcoat pockets, were taken from him. He was formerly a hairdresser, and is remembered to have exercised his profession at Brighthelmston, about nine years since.

### February 26TH 1787

Last Thursday se'nnight, as the Fletching carrier was going with his cart to London, he was stopped about five in the morning a little beyond the White Horse, on the Wash Way, by three footpads, two of whom clapped each a pistol to his breast, while the other rifled his pockets and took from him 19s, in money and his pocket book containing orders and a letter that enclosed two drafts from Mr George Beard, of Chailey, one for £150 drawn at six days and then payable and the other for £25 which was not payable for some time, Mr Beard, on hearing of the robbers, went immediately to London to stop payment, but unfortunately the robbers were before him, having forged the indorsement on the first mentioned bill and received the cash for it. The carrier was not apprized of the contents of the letter or he would have put it in a more secure place than his pocket book. The carrier had with him a little boy, his son, who, seeing his father so roughly attacked, cried, when one of the cowardly villains also clapped a pistol to his breast to quiet him. They made off across the fields to London.

### February 11TH 1788

On Tuesday as the woman who collects the tolls at Brayle Place turnpike gate was sitting with her daughter before the fire, a man with two handkerchiefs tied about his head and the underpart of his face blackened in order to disguise him, rushed in upon them and demanded of the woman her money. She replied that she had none of her own, and that which was not hers he should not have. Whereupon he drew out a pistol and presented it at her head, which she with astonishing intrepidity and presence of mind pushed aside, and seizing him by the collar at the same instant, attempted to push him out of doors. But before she had effected it, a man (a lodger) who was asleep in the house, alarmed by their noise, came to her assistance, when the villain was soon overpowered and obliged to decamp without his booty. Such courage and resolution in a woman are rarely met with.

### May 26TH 1788

About five o'clock on Tuesday morning last, as James Dann, of St John's Common, a dealer in fish, was returning home with his cart from the London markets, he was stopped on the road, between Peace-porridge Gate and Crawley, in this county, by two footpads, armed with pistols, who robbed him of £93, and then made off with their booty. The money was deposited in the cart, where there was also another parcel of cash, which the robbers luckily did not discover. They wore round hats, with their hair tied behind, and one had a blue and the other a brown coat with dark round-frocks over them.

["Peace-porridge" is the hamlet of Pease Pottage.]

### August 11TH 1788

On Monday night last, between 10 and 11 o'clock, as Mr. Chitty, a linen-draper of Lewes, was returning home from Brighthelmston races, in a single horse chaise, he was stopped on the road, between that place and Falmer, by three highwaymen, who robbed him of a metal watch and a guinea and a half in money, and got clear off with their booty.

The same night one of the Brighthelmston stage waggons belonging to Messrs. Bradford and Company, was robbed of a truss, containing cambricks to the amount of near four hundred pounds as it was going out of town, which was effected by cutting a hole in that part of the tilt, near to which the truss was deposited. Early the next morning the truss was found concealed in a dunghill, near this town; it had been opened, but on examination there appeared to be only one piece missing, which was also found on Wednesday by some schoolboys, together with a bunch of picklock keys, hid in a clump of stinging nettles on Church Hill.

The circumstances of finding the truss was wisely kept a secret for several days, during which time some persons were properly placed to watch the spot where the stolen property had been concealed, in expectation that the robbers would return to it for their booty; hut not having done so, a man suspected to be concerned in the robbery was on Saturday taken up and examined before two Magistrates in this town, who committed him to the house of correction here for further examination.

### August 18TH 1788

The man who was last week taken up on suspicion of robbing the Brighthelmston waggon, was on Friday examined, when nothing positive deduced against him, he was discharged.

### February 23RD 1789

One day last week, a young man, a farmer near Chichester, who had been to that city to recover a legacy of £100, on his return home with the cash, etc., in his pocket, was stopt near Lavant, by two men and a woman who attempted to rob him. One of the men struck at him and at the same time made an effort to seize his horse's bridle, but the beast starting in consequence, the villain missed his aim, which the young man had the presence of mind to take advantage of and clapping his spurs to his horse, galloped off and thereby saved his property.

About 8 o'clock on Tuesday evening last, as Daniel Warner of Dane Hill, near Lewes, was on his return home from Lewes on horseback, he was stopped in the parish of Chailey not far from Sheffield Bridge, and robbed of his watch, and above fourteen shillings, by two persons who are supposed to be chimney sweepers. Proper means not having been used in due time, the culprits are not yet taken. They were tracked a considerable distance by the impression left on the road from their shoes, one of which was remarkable having lost half of the iron with which the soal was plated.

## November 29TH 1790

On Monday last, between 6 and 7 o'clock in the evening, as Mr. Dulot, bookseller, on the Steine, Brighton, and Mrs. Richards, of the same place, were on their way to London in a one horse-chaise, they were stopped on Staplefield Common, between Cuckfield and Handcross by two highwaymen, who robbed Mr. Dulot of between 4 and 5 guineas and his watch, but made no demand on the lady. As soon as they had secured their booty, they made off towards Cuckfield, and were recollected by the keeper of Slough Green turnpike to have passed through that gate after the robbery. One of the highwaymen was mounted on a black horse, and dressed in a brown coat.

## November 26TH 1792

One day last week about 6 o'clock in the evening, as the shepherd of Sir H. Goring, of Highden, in this county, was returning home after having folded his flock, he was stopped on the Downs by three foot-pads, two of whom held pistols to his head, while the third rifled his pockets of three guineas in gold, and eight shillings in silver.

Same day a private soldier, belonging to the 11th regiment of Light Horse, was stopped by two fellows near the Pad, at Lancing, who clapped a pistol to his breast, and with horrid imprecations demanded his money, which the soldier gave them to the amount of three halfpence. The dragoon, who was without his sidearms, having suspected the footpads' intent, before they had closed with him, took his watch from his fob, and dropped it by the road side, and thereby fortunately saved that part of his property.

Two attempts on two successive nights have been lately made on the house of Mr. Marchant, of Beeding, in this county, by some villains whose noise had both times created an alarm in that family, that obliged them to decamp without effecting their purpose.

One day last week two men carrying a wallet at their backs, went to the house of Mr. Soper, a farmer, at Henfield, in this county, and asked charity at the door; but finding there was no person in the house but a maid servant, they demanded of her provision sufficient to fill both their bellies and their wallets; and in an authoritative voice that much alarmed the girl, till her master appeared in sight, which relieved her from her apprehensions, and occasioned those sturdy beggars to decamp with the utmost precipitation.

### December 3<sup>RD</sup> 1792

Last Saturday se'nnight in the evening one Peter Lillywhick, a labouring man, was stopped on the high road near the town of West Tarring in this county, by two footpads, who robbed him of eleven shillings, which he had just before received of Mr. Markwick of that place for his week's work. He afterwards went back to Tarring and gave the alarm, when two Light Dragoons, armed, with their carbines, very properly accompanied Lillywhick in pursuit of the robbers, and had not been long out before they discovered a man with some geese a little distance from them, but on seeing the soldiers, he dropped the geese (which he had stolen) and took to his heels. One of the dragoons fired at him in his flight, but without effect.

## December 10<sup>TH</sup> 1792

Last Friday morning Mr. Thomas Guy, of Chiddingly, was knocked down and robbed of his watch and money as he was foddering his father's beast by a fellow in a sailor's dress. The robber was, however, soon afterwards traced by his footsteps (which were marked by the particular manner in which his shoes are plated) to the Half Moon on Heathfield Down, where he was taken with the watch in his possession He was the same day committed to Horsham Jail, in order to be tried for the offence at our next Assizes.

## July 29<sup>TH</sup> 1793

On Wednesday morning last, the boy carrying the Strood mail, from Horsham to Strood, was stopped on Farthing Bridge by three footpads, one of whom held the horse, another rifled the bag, and took thereout a newspaper, there being no letters, and the third forcibly took a cap from the boy's head; but as the words Strood Mail are written thereon, it will probably lead to a discovery of these atrocious offenders.

## October 5<sup>TH</sup> 1795

On Friday se'nnight about the dusk of the evening, as Mr. Martin of Plumpton Green, near this town, was returning on foot from Brighton to the place of his abode, accompanied by his son, a little boy, they were overtaken about three miles from Brighton by a man in a soldier's red uniform who at first entered into conversation with Mr. Martin, but shortly afterwards took an opportunity of stepping behind him and by a violent blow on the back of his head struck him to the ground, and was proceeding to rifle his pockets but Mr. Martin, who was not entirely deprived of his senses by the blow, soon recovering his legs, assaulted the rifleman in his turn, and after a violent conflict in which a considerable quantity of blood was lost by both parties, got the original assailant under him, and would certainly have secured him but for the piercing cries of the little boy, which so powerfully excited his parental concern that he quitted his prostrate foe, and whilst administering comfort to his affrighted child, the villain escaped.

## 10TH April 1797

Last Wednesday evening as Mr. Tugwell, shoemaker of Glynde, was returning home from Ditchling Fair on horseback, he was accosted by two footpads, who rushed from a bridge, seized his horse's bridle and with horrid imprecations demanded his money; but by clapping spurs to his horse, he fortunately got off without being robbed.

## February 12TH 1798

The following daring robbery was committed a little before noon, on Thursday last:

As Charles Scrase Dickens, Esq., of Brighthelmston, High Sheriff for this County, was returning home from London, with his family, his carriage was stopped, about three miles out of town, by a single highwayman, who clapped a pistol to the head of Mr. Dickens's child, and demanded of the gentleman his money, who gave him nine guineas and his watch, with which the robber rode off. He was a young man of very genteel appearance, and received his booty with a trembling hand.

## January 27TH 1800

Whereas it has been represented to the Commissioners of His Majesty's Customs that, on the 3rd of December last, between the hours of nine and ten o'clock at night. as THOMAS PELHAM, a Riding Officer, in the service of the Customs at Brighton, within the Port of Shoreham, was returning home coastwise, on horseback, from duty, he was met by EDMUND DAVEY, of Rottingdean and another Person, near Black Rock Bottom, who told the Officer that a little further he would see three people stuck up, or near Hobden's Mill, and desired him to tell them to come along; that the Officer wished them a Good night and proceeded on, and immediately afterwards he was stopped by three persons, who, upon his asking their meaning, struck at him with their bludgeons, and said to him "Damn your eyes, we have got you, and will kill you on the spot", but the Officer got from them, and rode away as fast as he could, the three men following him, 'till they came near Brighton, crying out "Stop him" and making use of dreadful imprecations; but a horse and man falling, the Officer escaped from them with the loss of his hat.

The Commissioners of His Majesty's Customs, in order to bring the offenders to justice, do hereby promise a reward of TWENTY POUNDS, to any person or persons, who shall discover and apprehend, or cause to be discovered and apprehended, any one or more of the said offenders, to be paid by the Collector of His Majesty's Customs at the Port of Shoreham, upon conviction.

By order of the said Commissioners of His Majesty's Customs.
HEN. PARTINGTON, Collector,
T. EDWARDS, Comptroller.

## KEEPING LAW AND ORDER

November 10TH 1783

On Friday last John Card was apprehended by a warrant from Lord Sheffield, charged with knocking down and robbing Mr. John Wille, on Chailey Common, of four guineas and some silver.

His Lordship having ordered his commitment to Horsham Gaol, the constable with his assistants, had conveyed him about two miles from Sheffield Place on his road thither, when the father and two brothers of Card assaulted them, and, attacking Mr. Kent, a farmer, who had been ordered to assist the constable, and who, with great spirit held the prisoner, they seized a pistol, which he, suspicious of a rescue, had borrowed from Lord Sheffield's park-keeper, and one of them fired it at Mr. Kent when close to him. Luckily his arm intercepted the ball, which lodged there, but the prisoner was rescued, and made his escape. Notice being given to Lord Sheffield, his Lordship was immediately at the place, and having raised the country people, by proper exertions, the father and two sons were severally taken, and the whole family committed before night, except the son who was rescued, but from the active and proper precautions which were taken, there is no probability of his escape. The family has been for some time the terror of the neighbourhood. The sons are remarkably fine men, and two of them have served in the Sussex Militia, in his Lordship's own company, and have behaved well, but during this summer had been guilty of several outrages. The ball has not yet been extracted from Mr Kent's arm.

## June 29TH 1785
### ADVERTISEMENT
Lancing Society. For Prosecuting Felons, Thieves, and others. The next general meeting of the Members of this society will be held at the house of James Farver, bearing the sign of the Sussex Pad, in the parish of Lancing, in the County of Sussex, on Monday the 6th Day of July next, at 11 o'clock in the forenoon. By order of the Society Henry Brooker, Clerk and Treasurer. Brighthelmston, June 27th 1789.

## May 12TH 1788
Late on Saturday night one of the caps and balls belonging to the stonework at Lewes Bridge was wantonly removed and thrown into the river, by some evil disposed persons. The constables yesterday used their endeavour to discover the offenders but without effect.

## June 19TH 1797
In the night of Sunday, the 11th instant, 4 Hen Turkey, with eleven young ones, seven Ducks, and a Hen with thirteen chickens, were stolen from the premises of Mr. Wm. Groom, of Edburton.

A reward of Seven Guineas will be given to any person that will discover the offender or offenders, to he paid on his or their conviction by Mr. Brooker, of Brighthelmston, Treasurer of the Lancing Society for Prosecuting Thieves. June 16, 1797.

## 11TH December 1797

Last Thursday night the rapper-stealers were again busied in the practice of their felonious profession, but their depredations this time were not confined to rappers only, for latches, lamps, ladders, bells, wall-brackets, and even hog wash tubs, were removed and despoiled by these nocturnal ramblers; who in cases of detection, might perhaps plead inebriation in excuse, but this would prove a flimsy one against a rigorous prosecution; which, to be serious, might possibly in such cases, inflict the punishment of transportation.

## February 4TH 1799

A Person, who has been upwards of 15 years employed in the managing different Poor-Houses in this County, and is perfectly capable of carrying on the manufacture of Woollen and Linen, is desirous of contracting to Farm the Poor of one or more Parishes, by the head, from Lady Day next, for a period of not less than 12 months; or of engaging as a Governor.

The most satisfactory reference can be given, as to the character of the Advertiser, and the good treatment the Poor have experienced that have been placed under his care.

For further particulars apply to Charles Levitt, Gardner Street, Hurstmonceux. Jan. 24th 1799.

## February 25TH 1799

For want of other amusements that of rapper-stealing has been introduced at Brighton, where in the course of last week, several were wrenched from the doors in different streets, and with as much success as the same species of fun was practised some time back in this town [Lewes] when the utmost vigilance was in vain exerted, to detect the nocturnal depredators.

## November 18TH 1799

On Tuesday evening, or early on Wednesday morning last, out of Mr. Tillstone's Goose house, at Moulscomb, near Brighthelmston, THREE old Geese, two young ditto, and a young white Gander; each of which had their right wing cut.

Whoever will discover the offender or offenders who stole the same shall. upon his or their conviction receive a reward of FIVE GUINEAS, to be paid by Mr. Tillstone, over and above the reward given by the Lancing Society for the prosecution of Thieves and other offenders.

## PRISONS

## March 3RD 1788

ADVERTISEMENT

Whereas William Geering of the Parish of Westham, in the County of Sussex, being under Prosecution for assaulting Pryor Breden, an officer of His Majesty's Customs, at Pevensea in Sussex, in the due execution of his duty, was some time committed to the Gaol of Pevensea aforesaid, for want of Bail: and whereas in the night of 3rd of December last, the said William Geering broke Gaol, and hath since absconded.

The Honourable Commissioners for His Majesty's Customs, in order to bring the said William Geering to Justice, do hereby offer a reward of £10 to any Person or Persons, who shall discover and apprehend, or cause to be discovered and apprehended, the said William Geering; to be paid upon his safe delivery again into the custody of the Keeper of the said Gaol.

The said Geering is a well-made man, strong and boney, has hazel eyes, black hair, remarkably straight, almost touching his shoulders, aged about 30 years; had on when he made his escape from Prison, a dark raven coloured coat, dark blue cloth waistcoat, dirty leather breeches, and dark worsted stockings, is a Carpenter by trade, and rather knock-kneed; he worked some years since at Rolvendean in Kent but last at Westham, aforesaid.

By order of the Commissioners,
Thomas Philip Lamb,
R. Butler. Custom House, Rye, 20th February, 1788.

### January 16ᵀᴴ 1792

At the general quarter sessions for the eastern part of this county, found guilty of grand larceny and ordered to be transported, Thomas Williams and Joseph Savage (the former aged 20, and the latter 25 years) for stealing two asses, the property of Edward Venis, of Burwash.

Savage, one of the two prisoners convicted of stealing jackasses, was so little affected by the sentence of exile pronounced against him that he immediately after began to bray in court, like one of those stolen animals, in derisive allusion, we may suppose, to his crime, and with a ghastly sneer observed to those around him that "It was a d—n hard kick from a jackass." He also swore at the principal witness, and wished to have him within his reach; and, if we may trust his physiognomy, the poor man could not well get into a more dangerous situation. He and his comrade in iniquity being tramps, many of their vagrant fraternity attended the trial and, we are sorry to say, escaped the notice of the police.

### February 6ᵀᴴ 1792

On last Friday night, the convicts and some other prisoners in Horsham jail formed a plan for their escape, which was fortunately discovered and prevented by a person who is also confined in the same prison. They wrenched the poker from the grate, to which it was chained, with a design to use it against the Turnkeys when they came on their nightly round. Their intention was to bind (if not kill) and strip them. Two of the party were next to put on the Turnkeys' clothes, pass thus disguised with their keys and lanthorn through the jailer's house, and open the gates for their accomplices.

It is scarce necessary to observe that Savage, the jackass stealer, who brayed so impudently at the Bench of Justice after he had received sentence of transportation, at our late sessions, was a principal in this desperate undertaking. But he and his party have been since chained and collared down, so as totally to put it out of their power to meddle a second time with the poker,

## February 13TH 1792

The merit of the discovery and disappointment of the daring plan lately formed by the convicts in Horsham jail. is due to one Rochester, who is also a convict in that prison. He opposed the adoption of it at first, for which his life was threatened. But he found it necessary to temporize until he heard the Keeper's approach, whom, at small risk to himself, he warned of the intended attack.

The Keeper has, with laudable gratitude, since exerted himself to procure this man liberty, and we wish he may prove successful in his application.

## November 2ND 1795

From the House of Correction in Lewes on the evening of the 27th October last, James Faulkner, alias Fackner. He is about 25 years of age, 5ft. 2ins. high, black eyes, dark complexion, dark hair, very short made, and speaks short. Who ever apprehends the said person and delivers him to the House of Correction shall receive two guineas reward, exclusive of all reasonable expenses.

## November 9TH 1795
### ADVERT

Whereas an advertisement appeared in last Monday's paper offering two guineas reward for apprehending James Fackner, who escaped from the House of Correction, Lewes; This is to give notice that his crime is neither murder nor felony, but for a bastard child by a common strumpet; he broke neither bars nor doors, but found them open and made the best of his way out.

## March 30$^{TH}$ 1795

A singular kind of theft was lately committed in the House of Correction in this town (Lewes); the keys of that prison, being a desirable acquisition to some, were actually stolen therein, and beyond the recovery of the keeper, who has exerted himself in the most diligent search for that purpose, and to trace out the thief, but hitherto in vain

## April 6$^{TH}$ 1795

The keys of the House of Correction lately stolen within that jail have not yet been recovered, nor has the thief been traced out; one of the prisoners named Butterfield, is however, strongly suspected, and in order to bring him to confession was after examination before a Magistrate ordered into solitary confinement.

## 5$^{TH}$ June 1797

Wanted. On or before the 1st day of September next a steady and industrious Man and his Wife, as Governor and Matron of the House of Industry of sixteen united parishes, of Easebourne, near Midhurst, in Sussex. The number of Paupers in the House is usually about 150. No persons need offer themselves who cannot be well recommended and who are not qualified to direct the diet and discipline of the family, and be able to keep the accounts.

Apply to No.4 Clifford Street, Bond Street, London; or to Mr. Tyler, at Petworth, Sussex.

## 11$^{TH}$ December 1797

Last Wednesday morning Samuel Jordon, a prisoner in our House of Correction (Lewes), was found hanging in his cell. He was committed only the day before, charged with stealing a sheep the property of Mr. Holford, of Clayton. He effected his rash design by means of his smock-frock, one end of which he fastened to the gratings of his cell, and twisted the other round his neck. He was found upon his knees. Coroner's verdict, lunacy.

## February 25<sup>TH</sup> 1799

A few days since, a conspiracy amongst five of the prisoners confined in Horsham Gaol. for divers felonies, in order to effect their escape, was luckily discovered by the Keeper. who was first induced to suspect their design by having missed an iron hasp from one of the ward doors. After a diligent search. the piece of iron above-mentioned, and rope made of bed-clothes, and other articles, necessary for their purpose, were discovered in an ash-hole; and after a strict examination of the suspected, one of them was brought to confess their whole design. which was to have murdered the Turnkey when he came to lock up, and afterwards to escape over the outside wall by means of the rope and piece of iron. The conspirators have been since properly secured in separate apartments.

## December 23<sup>RD</sup> 1799

One day last week a man apparently in great distress. went to the house of a farmer named Warren, in the neighbourhood of Petworth, and asked permission to sleep in his barn. a request which the farmer humanely and very readily complied with. The next morning one of his servants, on going to work, was surprised at seeing a sow and seven pigs, which were kept in a small close before the barn, without a tail among them every one having been docked close to the rump! The man having communicated the odd circumstance to his master, suspicion immediately alighted on the mendicant as the perpetrator; and to the barn they directly went, where they found him busied in threshing corn: on asking him what he was about and what he had been doing? he answered that "he had had, during the night. a severe engagement with the sow and her family: that he had conquered and brought spoils (exhibiting the tails!, and was then knocking out a little corn for the discomfited enemy!"

*Bourne Street, Hastings, c1828*
*On the left is the George Inn, in the centre the gaol with the stocks and whipping post, and on the right the theatre, later a Wesleyan chapel*

Mr. Warren immediately took the man before Lord Egremont, to whom it clearly appeared his senses were greatly deranged; insomuch, that it could not be discovered. from his examination. whence he came or to whom he belonged. His Lordship, however, to prevent further mischief, committed him to Petworth House of Correction.

## March 10TH 1800

Whereas John Baker (otherwise Green), effected his escape in the night of the 2nd of this instant March, from the Common Gaol in the town and port of Hastings. in the county of Sussex, to which Gaol he was committed for Felony.

The said John Baker, alias Green, was born in the parish of Hollington, in the said county, is about twenty-two years of age, about 5 feet 8 inches high; sallow complexion; short brown hair;

speaks slowly and with a little impediment in his speech, rather blear eyed; a small cut on the right side of his face, and has a hurt on his left hip.

### June 2ND 1800

Broke out of the House of Correction, at Lewes, in the County of Sussex, on Tuesday, the 27th day of May, instant:

RICHARD TELLING, the younger, late of STOCK-FERRY, in the parish of Piddinghoe, near Lewes, aforesaid, who at the last General Quarter Sessions for the Eastern Division of Sussex, was sentenced to be confined until he could find sureties of the peace towards THOMAS CARR, of Beddingham, Esq., the High Sheriff of the County of Sussex, for the space of two years.

The said Richard Telling is a tall thin man, of the age of 30 years or thereabouts, light complexion, light brown hair, which he wears loose and long, slender made, dull heavy countenance; by trade, a shoemaker; formerly in the Sussex Militia, and has lately followed his trade of a Huckster, in buying fish at the seaside, and retailing them in the country, is well-known to the smugglers on the coast.

Whomsoever will apprehend the said Richard Telling and lodge him in any of His Majesty's Gaols, and give information thereof at the House of Correction at Lewes, shall receive a reward of Twenty Pounds, from me.

WILLIAM CRAMP, keeper.

## PUNISHMENT

### March 23RD 1778

On Wednesday the Assize for this county ended at East Grinstead, at which two prisoners were capitally convicted and received sentence of death, viz. William Harris, for robbing Hyam Solomon, a Jew on the highway and William Snashall, for horse stealing. They were both reprieved before the Judge left the town.

William Dillaway for assaulting Henry White and William Grice, Mariners, belonging to the Chichester Custom House Cutter, in the execution of their duty, and rescuing from them a quantity of prohibited goods which they had before legally seized, was sentenced to 7 years hard labour on the River Thames.

James Jackson, otherwise Watson, for robbing Abraham Zachariah, in Poling Wood, near Arundel, acquitted.

### July 14<sup>TH</sup> 1788

The Commission of Assize at Horsham. William Still, found guilty of two indictments one of which was for stealing a gelding, the property of Henry Ford, of Henfield, the other for stealing a mare, the property of one Earl of Hamfly, near this town [Lewes]. The Judge having informed Still that it was his intention to make an example of him to warn others, from the commission of similar offences, exhorted him to make a proper use of the little time he had to live, and particularly to make a discovery of those who had been concerned with him, observing that he must have had accomplices, as crimes of this nature were rarely committed by one alone.

### July 28<sup>TH</sup> 1788

Last Saturday William Still who received sentence of death at our last assizes for horse-stealing was executed at Horsham pursuant of his sentence. His coffin was being placed in the cart with him, he rode on it to the place of execution, where he appeared totally unmindful and insensible of that great and awful change he was about to experience. He seemed to pay no kind of attention to the clergyman who prayed by him, and stepped on his coffin to receive the halter about his neck with a degree of impenitance which shocked the surrounding multitude. He had nothing to say under the gallows, but on being asked by the gentleman who officiated for the Sheriffs, if he was guilty of the crime for which he was just going to suffer he replied "Yes" when the cart was drawn from under him and he was launched into eternity. Had not the malefactor himself been so insensible of shame, his sufferings must have been much augmented by the indecency of the executioner, who, to his infamy be it spoken, appeared at the gallows so beastly drunk that to maintain his feet he was frequently obliged to lay hold of the poor wretch he was preparing to execute and whose dying moments were prolonged by the bungling manner in which he performed the fatal office.

### July 18TH 1791

The grand jury at the general quarter sessions at Horsham, found against William Sherlock, a bill of indictment charging him with being a profane swearer, and with having destroyed the stocks and whipping post erected for the better security of the peace and honesty of the said parish.

### October 10TH 1791

At the general quarter sessions at Petworth, William Sherlock found guilty of pulling down and destroying the common stocks of the parish of Cowfold, was ordered to be left in hard labour, in the Petworth House of Correction, for the space of one month.

### January 16TH 1792

Last Wednesday a man was conveyed from the house of correction in this town [Lewes] to Brighton, and there publicly whipped at the market place, by order of our magistrates, for pawning some linen his wife had taken to wash. It was a sight which never before occurred in that town within the memory of the present generation. Though the man's crime and character fully justified the sentence, it is to be regretted that the Pawnbroker's Act, or any other, should expose a Briton, who still boasts himself free, to so degrading and severe punishment, without appeal to his country in a Court of Record or having his criminality ascertained by his peers.

### January 23<sup>RD</sup> 1792

Last Saturday, William Ready and Samuel Vulgar, convicted of petty larceny at our last Sessions, were publicly whipped, according to their sentences, at the market post in this town [Lewes]. The former received 160 lashes, the latter 60.

Vulgar, after he had received his punishment, was taken into custody by a Sheriff's officer, who under authority of a Judge's warrant, attended for that purpose, the prisoner being charged with violently assaulting and beating an officer of the customs at Arundel while in the execution of his duty.

### 29<sup>TH</sup> October 1792

Last Saturday a man from Seaford who had been exchequered about two years ago for converting to his own use a part of a pipe of brandy, which the sea had driven on shore at the above place, was committed to Horsham gaol, being unable to satisfy the demands which have in consequence been made upon him. His case is rather a harsh one, having some time since raised friends to pay upwards of £60 for him, and which he considered as a composition of the whole sum he had been exchequered for.

### November 5<sup>TH</sup> 1792

Last Saturday se'nnight a boy was convicted before the Mayor of Chichester of driving a wheelbarrow on the new pavement in that city, on the information of a Commissioner, and was fined accordingly, but being unable to pay the fine himself, his father, who is a man of property and was present, 'twas expected would pay it for him; but this he positively refused to do, alleging that it was cruel to enforce the law so vigorously against a neighbour's pocket; and to save his cash, actually left his son to the mercy of the Mayor and the informant; but the latter unwilling that the boy should suffer the disgrace of a prison, through his father's inflexibility, generously paid the fine for him; and thus, having very properly enforced the law, made himself the first object of its punishment for the example of others.

## September 15<sup>TH</sup> 1794

A circumstance occurred a few nights ago at a Public House at East Grinstead, which had nearly produced consequences that would have made mine host pay dear for his temerity:

A little mob of girls and boys, who conceived that they had not been fairly dealt by concerning some wax figures that had the same evening been disposed of by way of lottery at his house, assembled before it, and became rather clamourous; upon which the Landlord seized his gun and fired twice over the heads of the little rioters with powder only; but that not proving sufficient to effect their dispersion—he loaded his gun a third time with shot, and rashly, fired among them, when one boy was wounded in the face and different parts of the body, but we are happy to hear not dangerously.

## August 1<sup>ST</sup> 1796

On Tuesday last we were concerned to see the good police of the town of Brighton disgraced by a mob of boys and girls, who had assembled for the purpose of carrying about the streets in effigy, a woman of that place who they alleged had too severely corrected one of her children, but these young peace breakers and their advisers should be told that they can have nothing to do with the private concerns of any family for whose conduct they are not accountable; and that had their disorderly and tumultuous proceedings fallen under the notice of the constable, he would in all probability have placed them, and deservedly, under the severe correcting of the law.

## 16<sup>TH</sup> January 1797

At the General Quarter Sessions for the Western part of this county, held on Tuesday last at Chichester, two prisoners only were arraigned on charges of felony, one of whom, viz. John Batteson, found guilty of stealing a pair of patent worsted hose, and a pair of worsted gloves of the value of ten-pence, the property of Mr. John Dendy, of Horsham, was ordered to be re-committed for the space of three months, to be twice publicly whipped on market-days within that time, and at the expiration thereof to be discharged.

## February 16<sup>TH</sup> 1797

At the General Quarter Sessions for the Western part of this county, held on Tuesday last at Chichester, two prisoners only were arraigned on charges of felony, one of whom, viz. John Betteson, found guilty of stealing a pair of patent worsted hose, and a pair of worsted gloves of the value of ten-pence, the property of Mr. John Dendy, of Horsham, was ordered to be re-committed for the space of three months, to be twice publicly whipped on market-days within that time, and at the expiration thereof to be discharged.

The other, James Knight, tried for stealing in the yard of John Mitchell, of Midlavant, one elm board, his property, was acquitted.

The rest of the business brought before the Court was of a trifling nature, and not worth recording.

## 10<sup>TH</sup> April 1797

One day last week a man named Badcock of Isfield, got drunk and beat his wife in a manner which incensed the other good wives of the parish, to such a degree that they immediately assembled, 17 in number, seized upon the masculine offender, and tossed him in a blanket 'till they were heartily tired of this discipline; after which they threw him into an adjacent horse-pond amidst the shouts of a little multitude, who had become spectators of this summary mode of punishing a bad husband.

## 19<sup>TH</sup> June 1797

Last Saturday a young woman who was brought by the Parish Officers of Chailey before a Magistrate in the town [Lewes] to swear a bastard child to a lad of about fifteen years of age, on being threatened with imprisonment, walked coolly from the office into the street, when she took to her heels and, though vigorously pursued by the two officers who had her in charge, she out-ran them and escaped, with her infant in her arms, to the no small diversion and satisfaction of those who witnessed the race.

## 9TH October 1797

At the Quarter Sessions for the Western Part of this County, held on Tuesday last at Petworth, there were only four prisoners for trial viz. William Boxall and Charles Searle, for stealing a quartern of Brandy in a glass bottle, the property of Mr. Gibbs, of Petworth, who were acquitted; and two girls for stealing a quantity of milk, from a farmer at Angmering, one of whom was committed, and ordered to be imprisoned a fortnight and to be once publicly whipped, and the other acquitted.

## January 15TH 1798

At the General Quarter Sessions for the Eastern Division of the County, John Towner, for stealing a sack, containing about three bushels of oats, the property of Messrs. William and Thomas Chambers, of Bletchington, was convicted of the offence for which he stood charged, and sentenced to seven years transportation. He was accordingly yesterday morning sent off for Horsham Jail, there to be kept in safe custody, until opportunity offers for embarking him on board some transport for Botany Bay.

## February 12TH 1798

Wanted. A GOVERNOR, to take the poor of the parish of Ticehurst, in the County of Sussex, from Lady-day next

Any person inclined to treat for them by the head or otherwise, are desired to apply, as soon as possible, to thee Churchwardens and Overseers of the Parish of Ticehurst aforesaid.

Ticehurst. February 5, 1798.

## May 18TH 1798

Last Saturday a Journeyman Carpenter at Brighton, who suspected his wife of being too familiar with one of the Band, belonging to the Derbyshire Militia, resolved on satisfying his doubts; under pretence of leaving home for the night, he accordingly put on his best suit, and after taking leave of his rib, set out on. his pretended journey. Her sparkling eyes flashed joy at his departure, and she soon communicated the happy circumstance to her beloved Orpheus, who lost no time, in stringing his lyre, and charming her with the force of his tunes; but sad to tell, the husband unexpectedly returned and interrupted the union, just as it was vibrating its sweetest chords, and so belaboured poor Orpheus, that it is thought he will never attempt to play the second part of the same tune.

### July 30TH 1798

At our Assize, which ended on Saturday last at Horsham, there were only four prisoners for trial, two of these were capitally convicted and received sentence of death, viz.:

William Eglin, for stopping and assaulting Ann Hilton, on the highway, in the parish of Bletchington, on the 14th May last, and there taking from her person a pair of linen pockets containing one shilling and ninepence, her property. And Thomas Hilton, for stopping and assaulting on the highway, near Steyning between four and five o'clock in the morning on the 11th June last Mary Young, and there robbing her of two cotton handkerchiefs, a pair of shoe buckles, two half crown pieces, one shilling and sixpence, her property. He was also indicted for committing a rape upon her body, and no bill was found by the Grand Jury, but having been convicted of the robbery before the return of that bill into Court, he was not tried for the rape. Eglin was reprieved before the Judge left the town. Hilton remains for execution and it is expected will suffer at Horsham on Saturday se'nnight.

### August 18TH 1798

Last Tuesday afternoon an encounter took place in Southover near this town [Lewes], between two Grenadier Officers of the South Gloucester Militia, in which one of them whilst unarmed (having thrown his sword sheathed upon the ground) received a cut on his left hand, in guarding his head from the sword of his adversary, who in the scuffle having his weapon broken, seized the grounded sword and renewed the attack, but with no material effect before he was knocked down by his antagonist; when a gentleman who was accidentally present, interfered and put an end to the combat. The affair has since been submitted to the consideration of a Court of Enquiry, the members of which adjudged that both parties should be sent to Coventry. This decision was succeeded by a challenge with pistols, but as no duel has in consequence taken place, we should hope that differences (which originated in a dispute about a hat intended to be worn at the Promenade Grove) has been amicably adjusted.

Since writing the above, and just as our paper was going to press, we learnt that one of the gentlemen, Mr. Rogers, had gratified his revenge by giving the other a sound drubbing, and sending in his resignation which has been accepted.

## December 10ᵀᴴ 1798

Whereas several persons have gone out a shooting on Sunday, in the parish of Ripe, and thereby horridly profaned the Lord's Day:—This is to give notice, that if any person or persons shall be found shooting or in pursuit of game or wild fowl on THE SABBATH, he or they shall be prosecuted according to the utmost rigour of the law. The Churchwarden, in the discharge of his office, and other principal inhabitants of this parish, are determined to inform, and put the law in force, against those that shall so presumptiously offend in future.

## February 18ᵀᴴ 1799

Whereas I, William Holden, have wantonly shot a bullet through the vane of Brighthelmston Church, and in consideration of my public asking pardon for this offence and paying the expenses incurred, the Minister and Churchwardens have stopped all further prosecution; I do hereby thank them for their lenity, and promise that I will not in future injure the property of any person, but endeavour by my good behaviour, to convince them of my sorrow for having thus offended.
William Holden. Witness, John Farmer.
Brighthelmston. Feb. 16.1799.

## April 1ˢᵀ 1799

At our Assizes which ended at East Grinstead, on Tuesday last, sixteen prisoners were tried, eight of whom were capitally convicted, and received sentence of death, viz.: William Drewett and Robert Drewett, brothers, for robbing the Arundel Mail, on North-heath Common. near Midhurst; Thomas Lucas, a boy, only thirteen years of age, employed as a letter sorter in the Post Office at Arundel. for stealing therein. a letter containing a draft, value Ten Pounds. the property of Mr. Mitchener; Edward Oram, for stealing in a field, in the parish of West Grinstead, a bay gelding, the property of Henry Hammond: George Fleet, for stealing in the parish of West Bourne, a black mare, the property of Thomas Pearce; Daniel Daniels, for stealing a colt, the property of John Whatford; John Elford, for stealing a mare, the property of James Freeman of Slinfold; and Philip Edwards, for a burglary and felony in the house of John Butt of Littlehampton.... The horse-stealers and Edwards, were all reprieved for transportation, before the Judge left the town. The Drewetts are left for execution. and are to suffer on North heath, as near the spot where they committed the robbery as the public convenience will admit of, where their bodies are afterwards to be hung in chains.

Thomas Lucas was respited, during his Majesty's pleasure, and we are in great hopes that the Royal clemency will be extended to his free pardon, as he was by both Juries recommended to mercy, and received a promise from the Judge to exert his utmost endeavours to obtain it.

The life of this unfortunate boy, it is lamentable to relate, became forfeited to the laws of his country, through the artful seduction of an infamous prostitute, mistress of a fruit shop at Arundel, who fitted him to her purpose by occasional drink, and a persuasion that his tender years would protect him from punishment. The abandoned woman, being by the prosecuting parties, considered only in the light of an accomplice. was admitted an evidence for the Crown, and thereby saved her own neck from the halter, as the Judge observed, she ought to have been indicted as the principal, which was the prevailing sentiment, as appeared manifest by the alternate pity and indignation of the whole Court. Mr. Sheppard, whilst pleading for the prosecution, was so affected, that he could not refrain from shedding tears.

## April 15TH 1799

Last Saturday. the unfortunate brothers. William and Robert Drewett, were executed on Horsham Common, pursuant to their sentence. at our last Assizes, for robbing the Arundel Mail. A report having prevailed that they were to be rescued on their way to the gallows, a strong military guard was placed at the outer gate of the Jail, about seven in the morning, soon after which the malefactors were brought out. and having ascended the cart, were escorted by the Military to the fatal tree, where Robert appeared much agitated and said nothing. William conducted himself with becoming fortitude, and persisting in his innocence, said, he hoped the sacrifice that was about to be made of him, would warn Jurors in future, from convicting innocent men; he then, apparently from exhortation, seemed more attentive to the clergyman who attended on the occasion, and after about 40 minutes spent in prayer, they were launched into eternity. William died without a struggle, but the convulsive twitches of Robert, exhibited life for some space of time after he was turned off. Their bodies after hanging the usual time, were cut down, and ironed, and then conveyed in a cart to North-Heath, and there hung on a gibbet 32 feet high, amidst at least two thousand spectators. for the accommodation of whom booths were erected as at a horse-race, or a cricket match.

## April 29TH 1799

Thomas Lucas, the misguided boy, who at the last Assizes was convicted of stealing a bill of Exchange from a letter. and condemned to be hanged, has since. Through the human intercession of the Judge, before whom he was tried. received his Majesty's free pardon. The woman who seduced him, has very properly been abandoned by all her friends and connections, to the poor-house, where it is to be hoped, she will find repentance in the bitter cup of reflection.

## October 14TH 1799

At the Sessions for the Eastern Division of the County, held at Lewes, John Smith, convicted of an assault on the person of Mary Barrett, in the parish of Westmeston, was ordered into solitary confinement for the space of two Calendar months, and during that time to be subsisted, sparingly, on bread and water.

## 2ND December 1799

Last week the weights at Southwick Mill were tried by the Constables of that district and found deficient 5lb in the cwt., at which the population were so irritated that they exhibited the Miller in effigy about the streets, and afterwards burnt it.

## December 9TH 1799

The Miller at Southwick, whose weights, upon examination, we in our last stated to have been found deficient; appears, after an investigation of the facts, not to have merited the obloquy, which has in consequence been cast upon him. The most respectable of his neighbours (together with the Constable who headed the inquisition) give him the character of a very honest man, and have signed a certificate to that effect. it is however certain that his weights were found deficient, though not to the extent as first reported; yet, if it be true, as stated, that he bought more than he sold by them, he must, if he intentionally defrauded his customers, at the same time have wittingly committed a greater fraud against himself which a fool or a madman only. could have been guilty of.

## March 24TH 1800

Whereas some wicked and evil disposed Boys, in the afternoon of Wednesday last, between the hours of three and four. by throwing stones from off the Eastern Cliff, did wantonly and maliciously KILL A SMALL DOG, belonging to a Lady of this town.—Now in order to discover the offender or offenders, a reward of TWO GUINEAS is offered, and which TWO GUINEAS, on the discovery of such offender or offenders, will be paid by Mr. DONALDSON, at the Library on the Marine Parade.

## April 14TH 1800

A few days since the Constables of Brighton, finding a quantity of new butter exposed to sale, that was deficient in weight, they seized the same, and distributed it amongst such of their poor, as they thought most deserving of it.

## April 21ST 1800

Last Thursday a private in the Westminster Militia, being detected in attempting to escape with goods which he had previously stolen in the shop of Mr. Heatherly, of Eastbourne, was the next day marched a prisoner to (Lewes) barracks, and there tried by a Court-martial, who found him guilty. and sentenced him to receive four hundred lashes, 125 of which were immediately inflicted, being as many as he was at that time able to bear, consistent with humanity, which, as in the present instance, should always be the attendant of executive justice.

## SERIOUS CRIME

### November 15TH 1779

Whereas a scandalous and infamous paper hath been stuck up against the Market House of this Borough [Lewes] by some wicked and ill-designed person, or persons, in the words and figures following,

G)      (Men if you will believe us

in)      (Advising you for your own good,

F)      (All you that have the least hand in trying to prevent the fire and fireworks in this town will come best off for it is determined betwixt us to have a fire of some sort, so if you will not agree to lett us have it in peace and quietness with wood and faggots we must certainly make a fire of some of your houses, for we don't think it is a bit more sin to sett your houses a fire and burn you in your beds, than it is to drink when we are thirsty. We don't do this to make a talk and a chavash about town only, but so sure as it is wrote on paper so surely God Almighty weare in earnest. For we should desire no better divertion than to stand at a distance and see your houses all in flames.

Gentlemen, we shall take no money nor anything else to go out of the square, for that is the place we have fixed on.

Now we do hereby offer a reward of twenty guineas to any person or persons, who shall inform against the offenders or offender, who actually wrote and stuck up the said paper, to be paid on conviction of such offender or offenders.

By us: WILLIAM ELLIS
WILLIAM JONES
Bailiffs.

### 23RD June 1783

Preston. Whereas a Report has, and still does prevail, that Charles Dennett, second son of Mr. Charles Dennett, late of Woodmancote, deceased, hath been guilty of Murder, for which there is not the slightest foundation. This is therefore to offer a Reward of Twenty Guineas if the Propagator of such Report can be known; which will be paid by Mr. Thomas Dennett, of Preston, upon full proof thereof.

N.B. – The said Report is supposed to originate about Southwick Green.

### 20TH November 1786

Last Thursday a trifling dispute happened between two young farmers on the road near Langley (near Eastbourne) respecting a dog, when a blow being exchanged, a scuffle ensued, in which one of them had his skull fractured by the other with the butt end of a horsewhip in a very terrible manner, 'Tis reported that he cannot live.

### March 3RD 1788

About a fortnight ago the following melancholy affair happened in the parish of Bramber in this county; a young woman of the place being with child delivered herself in her father's house of a female infant, which (shocking to relate) she immediately afterwards murdered by cutting its throat and then buried it in the garden.

## March 2ND 1789

One day last week some gypsies enticed away a child about 6 years old belonging to Mr Reed, plumber, of Chichester; they were proceeding with it out of the city with great expedition when a woman who saw them pass by, and who happily knew the child, immediately followed them and brought it back They had made the little innocent quite dirty, and enticed it away by the trifling reward of a cake; it is with great concern that we inform the public that these vile wretches escaped unpunished.

## May 10TH 1790

The present high price of wheat threatens serious consequences in this county. On Tuesday last, between one and two hundred of the peasantry assembled, and with large sticks in their hands, went in a body to Petworth, where they complained heavily of the exorbitant price of flour, saying that the gallon loaf, which some of their families consumed in a day, cost them 14$\frac{1}{2}$d., nearly the amount of their day's earnings, which rendered it impossible for them to support themselves and their families by honest industry, that they might as well be killed at once as starved to death, and added, they would have flour cheaper (as there was no scarcity) or they would grind the miller. Such we are informed is the kind of language in which they stated their grievance.

Mr. Johnstone remonstrated with them on the impropriety of their conduct, read the Riot Act, and gave them the Assize of Bread. After this they repaired to a baker's shop, and bought some loaves, which they weighed and found deficient. The baker was fined accordingly, and the informants received the penalty which they spent at the Angel Inn, and afterwards departed and dispersed, without doing the least mischief; but not without having first declared their intention of assembling again very shortly.

Though the temper of the mob on Tuesday was such as did not create much immediate alarm, yet it has laid a foundation for future apprehensions, as we hear a serjeant's guard has been since applied for to be kept constantly mounted in the neighbourhood of Petworth. But as all must agree with Blackstone, that preventive justice is upon every principle of reason, of humanity, and of sound policy is preferable in all respects to punishing justice, we hope the legislative power will take the matter into their consideration, and by removing the cause, prevent its effects. In the meantime we most seriously recommend it to the malcontents to remain peaceable, and on no account whatever have recourse to the very dangerous expedient by which they so unlawfully distinguished themselves on Tuesday last at Petworth.

## 1ST May 1797

At Slinfold Fair, on Easter Tuesday, a number of the military from Horsham Barracks behaved extremely riotously; they tore down the stalls, drove the countrymen away from the fair place, took possession of the only public-house in the place, ordered a large quantity of beer and other liquors for which they refused to make the landlord the smallest compensation, and finally broke all the mugs and other crockery they could find about his premises. On their return, a number of them broke open the door of a public-house at Broadbridge Heath.

## 7TH May 1798

About five o'clock on last Saturday morning, a fire was discovered to have broke out through the roof of the kitchen belonging to the Prince's Pavilion at Brighton. The Commissioners offer a reward of Two Hundred Guineas for the apprehension and conviction of the offender or offenders.

## January 21ST 1799

About seven o-clock on the evening of yesterday se'nnight, a poor negro man, was by his groans, discovered lying some little distance from the turnpike road. near Cowfold, in the agonies of death, by Mr. Gregory, of Henfield, who being unable to afford him any assistance. made the circumstances known at the Crabtree public house, about a mile distant, the landlord of which, with a degree of humanity that did credit to his feelings, immediately sent two men with a horse and cart to fetch him to his house, that proper care might be taken of him: but they had scarcely placed him in the cart, before he expired.

The deceased had frequently visited that neighbourhood as a beggar, and went by the name of William Thompson. At his death, only twelve pence were found about him but it is said at Horsham that at the commencement of the late Bank there. he placed fifty pounds at interest therein.

## November 11TH 1799

Last Tuesday evening proving wet, the anniversary of the Powder Plot was commemorated in the Cliffe, on Wednesday evening. when some mischievous person fixed a lighted squib to the waistcoat of a lad named Fowle, whereby he was so dreadfully burnt, that he now lies in a distressing, if not dangerous state.

On the same evening a number of lighted squibs were cowardly thrown at a poor, defenceless servant girl, who in consequence had her gown (which she could ill afford the loss of) partly burnt from her back, and her person placed under such alarm and fear that she was for some hours after in strong hysteric fits.

## December 2ND 1799

On Monday morning last a barn and large wheat rick, belonging to Mr. Holmes, of the Old Salts Farm, in the parish of Lancing, near Shoreham, were discovered to be on fire; and, notwithstanding the active exertions of a number of neighbours to extinguish the flames, upwards of 14 loads of wheat and other effects, amounting together to more than £500 value were totally consumed.

There is too much reason to believe that the above conflagration was wilfully occasioned; and we trust the means now using to discover the offender or offenders, will be attended with success; as we know of no offence so highly tinctured with depravity, so mischievous in its effect, and so richly meriting the most exemplary punishment.

## December 9TH 1799

Whereas a Barn, on the Old Salts Farm, at Lancing, In Sussex, full of Oats, with a Wheat Rick, and a Hay Rick contiguous. were in the night, between the 25th and 26th inst. wholly consumed by fire, and there is the greatest reason to think the said Barn was maliciously set on fire. We, therefore. whose names are hereunder written (inhabitants of Lancing aforesaid) do hereby offer a reward of ONE HUNDRED POUNDS to any person who shall give such information to John Holmes at Arundel; or Robert Holmes, at Lancing aforesaid, as shall be sufficient to convict or shall lead to the conviction of the person or persons who committed the said felony (except the person who actually set fire to the said barn) will discover his or her accomplice or accomplices therein, he or she will not only be admitted an evidence, and thereby secure a pardon, but shall also be paid the reward of One Hundred Pounds.

> J. M. Lloyd
> John Holmes
> Wm Willes
> Jas. Penfold
> John Grinsted
> James Lee
> Wm. Dabbs

November 30, 1799.    Sarah Carver.

## February 3RD 1800

Considerable rewards were last week offered to several places in this county, for the apprehension of persons who had dropped letters threatening to burn corn-stacks and houses, if flour was not speedily reduced to a moderate price. The Hampshire paper, of last week, exhibited a very audacious letter of a similar kind.

## February 24TH 1800

On Monday last about fifty labourers assembled at Petworth, and complained to the Magistrates of that district, that, in consequence of the excessive price of bread and other provisions, they, and their families were in a state bordering on starvation, notwithstanding their utmost industry used to support them. Sir Godfrey Webster, who was on a visit at the Earl of Egremont's, after patiently hearing the men's complaints, sent summonses to the officers of the parishes from whence the labourers had assembled, ordering their attendance before the Magistrates the next bench-day: after which the men quietly returned to their respective homes.

## May 19TH 1800

Whereas on Sunday last. about three o'clock in the afternoon, THREE STACKS of FURZE, belonging to me, containing 5,800 Faggots were by some means set on fire, and the whole nearly consumed, which if done by accident, by youth of either sex, who will confess to same, shall be forgiven and rewarded for such confession; but if wickedly and maliciously set on fire, I do hereby offer a reward of FIFTY POUNDS, to any person or persons. who shall discover the same, to be paid on conviction of the offender or offenders, over and above the reward offered by the Boreham Society for discovering thieves, felons, etc. FRANCIS HOLLAND Wartling, May 9, 1800.

## SMUGGLERS

### June 20TH 1774

Yesterday sen'night Mr. Wildman, Excise Officer at Cuckfield, having information of some smuggled goods which were laid up near Pease-Pottage Gate, a little distance from Crawley, he with two Dragoons, went and made a seizure thereof, but by the time they had loaded it on their horses a body of smugglers came to the spot, and made a demand of the goods, which Mr. Wildman not complying with, they immediately knocked him off his horse, when a warm engagement ensued. wherein the soldiers kept a continual discharge on the smugglers from their pistols till their ammunition was totally exhausted, when they immediately drew their swords, and four of the smugglers having then got Mr. Wildman down in a dyke, one of the soldiers went with a drawn sword to his assistance, with which

*The George Inn, Crawley*

he made a push at the smuggler's body, which the man luckily evaded, and turning about knocked down the soldier, but the other coming up at this instant made a violent blow with his sword at the smuggler's head, but striking below his mark, the man received a dangerous wound on his shoulder; another smuggler was terribly cut across the thigh, and 'tis reported one lost his life. However, they at last gained the victory and sent the officers and dragoons home with broken heads and otherwise terribly bruised, while they marched off.

### December 2$^{ND}$ 1776

Early on Tuesday morning last, some Revenue Officers, assisted by a party of Dragoons, seized, near Friston Mill in this County, upwards of 17cwt of tea and 9 casks of Geneva. The smugglers soon after returning to rescue the above seizure, were fired upon by the soldiers, who killed two of their horses and dangerously wounding a man, obliged them to desist.

### June 8TH 1778

On Monday as some smugglers were riding furiously through Lewes, one of them, being very drunk, guided his horse on the pavement, where he instantly slipped up, and falling with great violence against a post, was killed on the spot; the rider was but little hurt; after this they went to Ditchling, where they behaved in a very unbecoming manner, and being pretty severely beat and twice routed by the townspeople, rode away threatening to set fire to the town.

### June 27TH 1779

On Friday morning, the 25th ult. Messrs. Norton, Baker, and. Stow, assisted by other Revenue officers, seized from a large gang of smugglers, near Henfield. 38 bags of tea, in consequence of which a scuffle ensued between some of the officers and smugglers, where-in one of the former got most unmercifully beaten. The goods were, however, the same morning safely conveyed to Shoreham Custom House. The next morning the said officers seized 16 bags of tea and 11 cases of liquor near the same place, and carried them to the Custom House.

### August 30TH 1779

We hear that recruiting parties of Major Holroyd's Corps of Sussex Light Horse will be in Lewes and other towns in this country next week. We are told the Major prefers smugglers, thinking they will make the best Light Horse. This gives then an excellent opportunity of recovering the good opinion of their country and shewing their bravery and spirit in a proper way. They are not to serve out of England, and only for three years, or during the war and cannot be drafted like other regiments. Their quarters are to be Lewes and Brighton.

### 1ST November 1779

William Humphrey and — Guildford, two fishermen who were

boarded by some Frenchmen from a small boat, and carried off, have, we are informed, lately been heard of by some smugglers, who bring advice home that they are now imprisoned in France, but that their boats and nets are taken proper care of, and will be returned to them, should their friends make interest sufficient for their liberties.

## April 10TH 1780

On Friday evening some of the men belonging to the Shoreham Custom House cutter fell in with a small party of smugglers laden near Hove, and on finding them unwilling to deliver their goods fired upon them and shot one horse dead upon the spot, and wounded another, upon which the smugglers delivered up their goods, and

## 11TH September 1780

Last Saturday one of the fishermen at Brighthelmston on being impressed, attempted to cut off his left hand, to prevent his being sent on board a man-of-war, which he so nearly effected, that it was thought a surgeon's assistance would be required to complete the amputation. He had been pressed before and made his escape.

## March 24TH 1783

At our Assizes held at East Grinstead, on Monday last the 17th inst., before Mr. Justice Ashurst, Thomas Rogers, a private soldier, in the 10th Regiment of Dragoons, and John Fisher, as Excise Officer, were tried for the wilful murder of Jonathan Godfrey, a smuggler, at Slaugham, in this county; Rogers having, as an assistant to the Excise Officer, shot Godfrey through the body with a pistol, in an affray with a party of smugglers when Rogers was found guilty, and received sentence of death, but was reprieved by virtue of a warrant under His Majesty's sign manual, and Fisher was acquitted.

## 11TH September 1786

We are informed that a few days since as some boys were getting nuts in a wood near the parish of Mayfield, they found concealed some casks which they supposed contained spirituous liquor and went with the information to a Revenue officer in the neighbour-hood, but he being from home, and his wife, reflecting on the old proverb which says, delays are dangerous, and being a spirited Cornish woman, furnished herself with arms and ammunition, went to the spot and made the seizure, and got it conveyed safe home to her husband's home.

### 15$^{TH}$ October 1787

Captain B—ll, who lately put the Brighthelmston fishermen under as much fear of being impressed in consequence of having hired a number of armed men, and given them the air of a press gang, was on Monday evening last fairly put to the rout by the fishermen's wives and daughters, who assembled in a considerable body, armed with mops, besoms, firepans, etc., and therewith pursued the captain so closely that he was obliged to make his escape out of the windows of several houses in which he had taken shelter; and by means thereof, reached a post chaise and four that was provided for him, and thus escaped the fury of the *victorious amazons*, who then returned peaceably to their respective homes, to congratulate their husbands and sweethearts on their happy deliverance.

### December 3$^{RD}$ 1787

On Monday morning last Messrs. Mandy, Baker, Belcher, Rye and Bredon, Revenue Officers, with four light dragoons, seized near the Red House, in Pevensey Bay, upwards of 200 casks of foreign spirits, and afterwards lodged the same in His Majesty's custom house at East Bourne.

Last Friday evening Messrs. Butler and Neeve, custom house officers, with five dragoons, seized on the Downs between Balsdean and Rottingdean, eight horses and 68 casks of foreign spirits, the latter of which they afterwards conveyed to Newhaven custom house.

### December 20$^{TH}$ 1787

Last Tuesday was tried before the Lord Chief Baron of the Court of Exchequer, at Westminster, an information filed by His Majesty's

*Rottingdean*

Attorney General, against a person of Fairlight in this county, for exporting wool out of the kingdom, when the fact being clearly proved a verdict was given in favour of the Crown for £732, being the penalty of 3s. for every pound weight of wool so exported.

And on Wednesday another information was tried in the said Court against another person of the same place, brother to the above, for exporting Wool and live Sheep out of the Kingdom when a verdict was also given in favour of the Crown for, £3,800 4s. being the full penalty on the information of the wool and sheep so exported.

The profits arising from the above pernicious practice, we hear, are so great that those concerned in it do not make less than £100 per cent clear of all expenses on wool; and a middling Ram has been known to sell at Bologne for *Fifteen guineas.*

[The illicit exportation of wool was never stopped by law. In Sussex it dated back to the thirteenth century or earlier. Wool smugglers were called "Owlers".]

## March 3<sup>RD</sup> 1788

One day last week Messrs Heasman and Roberts, Custom House Officers, seized 96 casks of foreign spirits, and two bales of double handkerchiefs, which they afterwards lodged in Arundel Custom House.

On Friday last Messrs Butler and Neeve, Revenue Officers, assisted by four light dragoons, seized in the parish of Hove two horses, 6 bags of tobacco and seven casks of foreign spirits.

The same night 40 casks of brandy, rum and geneva, were seized near East Groyne, at Brighthelmston.

Last Friday some hundred gallons of spiritous liquors that had been legally seized at different times by Revenue Officers, were poured into the kennel in the public street of this town, and this day, we hear, several thousand gallons more are to share the same fate, in conformity to an Act of Parliament, passed for that purpose.

## April 14<sup>TH</sup> 1788

A few days since Messrs Butler, Neeve & Walter, Revenue Officers, seized at Rottingdean 71 bags of tobacco, 185 gallon casks of foreign spirits, and one horse with his furniture. The tobacco and spirits they afterwards conveyed to Newhaven Custom house.

## April 21<sup>ST</sup> 1788

Yesterday se'nnight the Revenue Officers at Seaford and East Dean seized near the piers at Newhaven, 120 casks of foreign spirits, one cask of Frontiniac, and two horses; and immediately afterwards the same officers seized in the hay 40 casks of spiritous liquors and two boats. The spirits they afterwards loaded in the Custom house at Newhaven and took proper care of the horses and boats.

Yesterday se'nnight an oyster boat, in coming into Shoreham harbour, took up at sea four casks of spirits and on showing the prize afterwards, one of the men agreed to take of the master half a guinea for his part, which he had no sooner received than he went on shore and lodged an information against the boat, in consequence of which a Revenue Officer went on board and seized both the liquor and the boat. The informer, on returning on board, underwent the discipline of a severe ducking, which was inflicted by tying a rope round his body and dragging him repeatedly through the harbour, for which he was occasionally compelled to pull off his hat and huzza, as an acknowledgment of the justice of the punishment he had received for his treacherous conduct. Many were present, and all applauded the nature and extent of his punishment.

### September 15TH 1788

On Saturday se'nnight were seized at Rye by the Revenue officers there, and a party of Light Dragoons, 66 gallons of brandy, and 84 gallons of Geneva.

Yesterday se'nnight Messrs. Froste and Waldin, Revenue officers, assisted by a party of Light Dragoons, seized near Arundel, 260 gallons of brandy, 105 gallons of rum, 196 gallons of Geneva, a boat, 2 anchors, and two warps, which were afterwards committed to the care of His Majesty's customs at Arundel.

The same day Messrs. Ragless and Duke, Revenue officers at Felpham, seized at Elmer, 28 casks of brandy and Geneva, and lodged the same in the Custom house at Arundel.

Last Wednesday a Revenue officer and two Light Dragoons seized at Bexhill, two horses heavily laden with tubs, from two smugglers, who afterwards tried to bribe the soldiers to restore their horses, but failing in this the soldiers having wisely resisted the temptation, they had recourse to more desperate means, that of breaking open the stable door, where the horses were in the night, and attempting to recover them that way; but one of the soldiers, a corporal, having reason to suspect their design, had laid himself up in the stable properly armed, and on the smugglers entering it, discharged his carbine at them, and shot one in the body; he was not dead when we received the information, but it was thought he could not survive, as the ball, which entered between the breast and shoulder, could not be traced to its lodgement consequently there could be little hope entertained of relieving the unfortunate man from its extraction.

## September 29TH 1788

The smuggler who was shot by the dragoon at Bexhill, is and now thought to be in a fair way of recovery.

A similar instance occurred last Week at Burwash Wheel, near Burwash. Mr Pudsey, Revenue officer, at Battle, having seized 15 casks of foreign spirits, and two or three horses, deposited the same, for present convenience, in a stable belonging to the Burwash Wheel public house, but where the seizure had not been long before the smugglers from whom it was seized appeared to retake it, which they attempted to do by forcing open stable door in the presence of the Officer who having expostulated with them in vain on the impropriety of their conduct, drew his pistol and shot one of the smugglers through the arm, after which he obtained the assistance of a peace officer, and thereby secured the seizure.

[Burwash Wheel, now Burwash Weald.]

*Hastings*

## October 6TH 1788

Last Saturday, in the afternoon, a tilted waggon, drawn by five horses, laden with prohibited goods, was seized on the road near Uckfield by Messrs. Palmer and Spencer, Excise Officers and a party of 15th Light Dragoons. The lading consisted of 9 casks of Cognac brandy, 22 ditto of Geneva, two bags of tea, and near 40cwt of tobacco. The carriage horses, liquors and teas were committed to the care of the Excise, and the tobacco was lodged in the custom house in Newhaven. The waggon and horses were the property of some person in Surrey.

## December 8<sup>TH</sup> 1788

Yesterday se'nnig one of the largest seizures that has been made for some time past on our coast fell into the hands of the custom house officer at Newhaven, Seaford and East Dean; it consisted chiefly of manufactured tobacco, and in quantity amounted to several tons weight, being the lading of a wagon, a cart, and 13 saddle horses, the whole of which the officers took full possession of and afterwards committed the same to the care of the customs at Newhaven. One day last week Messrs. Heasman and Roberts, Revenue Officers, seized 2 casks of brandy and Geneva which they afterwards lodged in His Majesty's custom house at Arundel.

## February 23<sup>RD</sup> 1789

Messrs. Belcher, Rye and Bredon, Revenue officers, assisted by two light Dragoons, lately seized near the Sluice, in the liberty of Hastings, 47 bags of tobacco, 5 bags of fine Souchong Tea, and two casks of foreign spirits, and lodged the same in his Majesty's Custom House at Eastbourne.

Early on Wednesday morning last Mr. Israel Medhurst, Revenue Officer at Newhaven, assisted by two Light Dragoons, seized near the pier heads, at that place, after a trifling skirmish, 9 fine horses, laden with 89 bags of tobacco and snuff, and 205 gallon casks of brandy and rum. The officer had seized another capital horse, but brought away only his bridle, which the smugglers had the address to slip over his head, and by means thereof saved a horse, which they valued above all the rest put together. The tobacco, snuff and spirits were lodged in Newhaven Customs House.

*The Blockade, Rye Harbour*

### 3ʳᴰ August 1789

In the night of yesterday se'nnight, a smuggling cutter was chased off Shoreham by a brig of the King's service, in which the cutter received many shots from the brig, that greatly disabled her rigging, notwithstanding which 'tis thought she would have got off, had not a calm come on, which gave the brig's crew an opportunity of manning their boats, and running long side the cutter, which they boarded, and took possession of. But the greatest part of her cargo the smugglers had thrown overboard.

### March 5ᵀᴴ 1792

On Friday last a Frigate, in the service of the Government, supposed to be the *Quebec*, hove in sight off Brighton, with two smuggling cutters in company, which she had fallen in with and made prizes of on Wednesday. Several ankers of spirits supposed to have been thrown overboard by the cutter's people while under chase, were on that day taken up at sea and brought on shore by the fishermen of the above place.

## May 28TH 1792

Early on Thursday morning last the Boat officers belonging to the Customs at Seaford, fell in with and took at sea, a little to the westward of Newhaven Piers, a lugger laden with 310 casks of contraband spirits, which were afterwards conveyed in safety to His Majesty's warehouse at Newhaven.

## July 16TH 1792

Last Monday three persons belonging to Henfield, one of whom is master of the White Hart Inn there, were committed by J. Aldridge Esq. to Horsham Jail, being charged on the oaths of two smugglers, or ten shilling men, with robbing them of their horses and saddles, which together with ten tubs of contraband spirits that they were laden with, the prisoner had taken from them and delivered into the possession of a revenue officer at Henfield, as his seizure.

["Ten shilling men" was the popular term of description of those who assisted smugglers in landing their goods, for which service they were paid 10s. per "run."]

## 15TH October 1792

Last Friday night a smuggling boat with four hands on board, belonging to Worthing, in a head gale of wind, was wrecked near Rottingdean Gap, and soon after dashed to pieces by the violence of the waves. The men on board were unhappily all drowned; and three of the dead bodies were the next morning taken up in Brighton. In the pocket of one of them was found eighty guineas. The same night a small vessel laden with apples, in making for Shoreham harbour, was driven aground off Southwick.

## December 3RD 1792

On Thursday last was tried in the Court of Exchequer at Westminster, a prosecution brought in the name of the Attorney-General, against Mr. John Liffen, a respectable brandy dealer of Hove in this county, in order to recover several penalties upon a supposed breach of the Excise laws, in having made use of several unentered rooms for the storing of his liquors.

The case, as represented by Mr. Farrar, and other officers of Excise, was, that they, by virtue of a search-warrant, went into Mr. Liffen's house and in several unentered rooms they found several parcels of foreign geneva, which they seized as forfeited.

On the part of Mr. Liffen it was proved, to the satisfaction of Court and Jury, that the liquors seized were at the time of seizure in the several apartments of, and belonging to, the lodgers of Mr. Liffen, who had purchased the same at Custom House sales, therefore the Jury found a verdict for Mr. Liffen.

## February 3ᴿᴰ 1794

On Friday night Mr. Collins, supervisor of Excise of this town [Lewes] was very roughly handled by two smugglers near Waldron, from whom he had seized four tubs of gin, but which they afterwards rescued leaving the officer for dead on the spot; but he soon recovered so as to be able to get to a neighbouring house, where he lay three days before he was removed home. However destructive the present war may prove to our commerce in general, there is one species of it, to which the war proves favourable, and that is our contraband commerce, for smuggling had not flourished for some years past, so much as at the present time.

## February 17ᵀᴴ 1794

On Thursday night Messrs. Hawke and Wentworth, officers of Excise, seized a cart and two horses laden with 24 casks of contraband spirits, which they had safely conveyed to the Excise office at Cuckfield. The cart had the appearance of being laden with fish, and was on its way to London when seized.

## March 3ᴿᴰ 1794

Yesterday se'nnight two men belonging to a smuggling cutter were drowned in coming to shore with a boatload of contraband goods, off East Bourne. 'Tis unknown by what accident they perished, and their boat soon afterwards drifted ashore, nearly full of water and with about half her cargo, which consisted of tubs of geneva. Their bodies were found on Tuesday morning near Pevensey. One unfortunate man left a young widow to lament his loss.

## May 12TH 1794

On Saturday, the 3rd instant, the *Swan* and *Swallow*, Revenue cutters, took at sea, a smuggling lugger, laden with 256 casks of contraband spirits, 31 barrels of snuff, and 2 ditto of tobacco and sent her into Shoreham.

The next day the same cutters fell in with and took a smuggling cutter laden with 400 casks of foreign spirits, and a quantity of tea, which they sent into Cowes.

## June 2ND 1794

Saturday last Captain Hawkins of Shoreham seized a smuggling cutter laden with upwards of 700 casks of foreign contraband spirits which he afterwards safely lodged in the Custom House at New Shoreham.

## August 25TH 1794

Last Wednesday morning Messrs. Lindsey and Geere, riding officers at Rottingdene, seized 51 tubs of Geneva which they found concealed in a cavern at Telscombe, made by the smugglers for that purpose. The officers plugged one tub and invited all the old women of the Parish to partake of it, which they helped to drink out, and some of them had sipped so largely of the enlivening extract that they soon found themselves stimulated, as if under the provoking influence of some powerful *diuretick*, and if one might judge from appearances, the liquor had suffered no diminution in its double distillation; it is however, not fair to say, that the good dames of Telscombe, conducted the process with as much modesty and decorum as their situation would admit of.

## October 20TH 1794

About ten days ago at Shoreham, some officers of the Prince of Wales (or 10th Light Dragoons) were returning to camp early in the morning when they observed a bottle on the beach, and on a nearer approach found it was occasioned by a gang of smugglers who were running a cargo of contraband spirits, whom they immediately attacked, and with the assistance of some soldiers from the camp secured the cargo till a Revenue officer arrived and made a legal seizure of it. It consisted of a boat and between four and five hundred tubs of geneva, which was afterwards lodged in his Majesty's warehouse at Shoreham. One of the boat's crew who showed an inclination to resistance, had his arm nearly cut off by a military officer, and, but for the gunwale of the boat, which stopt the progress of the sword, 'tis thought he must inevitably have been killed.

The smugglers had not long before made an attempt to land some goods in Newhaven, but were prevented by perhaps a too precipitate look out of some Revenue officers.

Two soldiers who were supposed first to have discovered the above mentioned tubs, took such inordinate draughts of the baleful spirit as rendered them incapable of getting far from the spot where the casks were deposited. They were both found the next morning lying dead drunk, below high water mark. One of them, belonging to the Artillery, never survived the shameful fit of intoxication in which he was taken up. He was generally esteemed a sober man, and was to have been married on the day he died.

### November 10TH 1794
In the boisterous night of Tuesday last some Grenadiers of the Sussex Militia found a tub of gin which the sea had washed on shore, when they immediately set it up on one head, and knocked in the other and then drank so immoderately of its contents that one of them named Thomas Tippin, a native of this town [Lewes] was found dead the next morning, near Hove; and another lying by him with but little signs of life. He, however, on having proper care taken of him recovered. The deceased had been often heard to express a wish that he might die drunk; he was gratified, and in consequence buried without any military honours being performed over his grave.

### November 10TH 1794
About five o'clock on Friday evening last as three smugglers laden

were riding through the town of Uckfield, one of them guided his horse on the pavement before the Maidenhead where a soldier was standing sentry, who to keep the horse at a distance charged his bayonet, which the smuggler disregarded at the peril of his life, and narrowly escaped with it, as the bayonet went through one of the tubs on which he was sitting, and set the liquor running about the street. Some of the soldiers pursued the smugglers, one of whom they overtook, and seized his horse and cargo.

## December 1ST 1794

Last Monday twenty one bags of tobacco containing about half a ton weight was seized at East Grinsted, in the waggon of Mr. Jarrat, carrier at Eastbourne on its passage to London, by an Excise officer who also made a seizure of the waggon and horses.

Tobacco is now become a very considerable article of contraband traffic. Perhaps not less than two thirds of its consumption in England are smuggled, and this is accounted for by the low price it bears, being less than would pay the duty on that which is called legally imported.

## December 8TH 1794

Last Tuesday morning, as a boat belonging to a smuggling cutter, was going on shore at Bear's Hythe, between Newhaven and Rottingdean, with about four hundred tubs of Genevas on board, the crew observed on the cliff some fires which had been made as a signal for them not to land; they accordingly put about their boat with the intention of returning to the cutter then lying in the road; but before they could reach her their boat shipped so much water from the great swell of the sea that the men on board were obliged to desert her on some person from the cutter who had discovered their danger, coming to their assistance. The boat afterwards drifted on shore, where she was dashed to pieces and her cargo made the legal plunder of Revenue officers, and the country people, each of whom is said to have come in for a good share of it.

## March 2ND 1795

The smugglers begin to prick up their ears in hopes that the additional duties on tea and spirits will give room for that revival of their contraband traffic.

A few days since Messrs. Ragless, Whitcomb and Lower, revenue officers, seized at Selsey, 60 casks of Geneva, and one ditto of tobacco which they afterwards conveyed in safely to his Majesty's custom house in Chichester.

## August 17TH 1795

The Custom House at Shoreham was a few nights since broken open and robbed of some property belonging to the Collector. The public money we hear was too well secured for the villains to lay their fingers upon.

## November 16TH 1795

On Tuesday the Stag Custom House cruiser, belonging to Rye, took at sea, off that place, a fine smuggling cutter laden with 500 nine and five gallon casks of foreign spirits and several bags of tobacco. One of the smuggler's crew was washed off the deck and drowned during the late blowing weather.

## Nov. 7TH 1796

Last Tuesday night Captain Haddock of the Stag Revenue cutter, belonging to Rye, took off Pevensey a smuggling boat laden with 600 tubes of contraband spirits and a quantity of tobacco, which he afterwards Landed and lodged in His Majesty's warehouse at the above place. The boat would have outsailed the cutter had there been wind enough to escape.

## May 8TH 1797

One evening last week a considerable quantity of contraband goods consisting of 181 pieces of silk handkerchief and a bag of tea was seized at Hawkhurst, Kent, in the Common Stage Waggon of Rye in this county on its passage to London; the waggon of course became forfeited; but horses, said to be worth £30 each, fortunately for their owner, in the stable at the time, consequently formed no part of Revenue Transfer.

## 8TH January 1798

A few nights since a private soldier belonging to the Derby Regiment of Militia, whilst on duty as a sentinel near Cuckfield, drank so inordinately of a tub of contraband spirits with which a smuggler was going past his post; that (on being relieved about ten minutes after) he laid himself down and almost instantly expired. The Coroner's Jury returned a verdict of *accidental death*.

## 3RD March 1798

A few days since some Revenue Officers made a seizure of tobacco and brandy, near Littlehampton, and having for the refreshment of their assistants, knocked in the head of one of the tubs, a Militiaman drank so inordinately of its contents that he languished to the next night, and then expired.

## March 12TH 1798

Last Wednesday, Mr. Cook, Excise Officer at Lindfield, seized near Haywards Heath, 52 bags of Tobacco in the leaf and conveyed the same to his own house, where it was safely deposited in his bed-room, 'till early on Friday morning, when a gang of smugglers, about twelve in number, beset the house, and after breaking the door and windows, rescued the greater part of it (upwards of 40 bags) which they effected by threatening the officer, until he had it thrown out of the window, when they loaded their horses, and rode off.

## April 9TH 1798

Last Thursday night as a gang of Smugglers were running a cargo of goods near Worthing, they were surprised by the crew of a Custom-house boat, who after some resistance on the part of the Smugglers, seized from them upwards of 300 tubs of contraband spirits, and a quantity of tobacco, which they safely conveyed in waggons to the Custom-House at Shoreham. The Boatmen also took three of the Smugglers' horses. The Smuggling Cutter, from which the above

*Winchelsea*

goods were landed, about a fortnight since, was 90 closely chased by the one in the service of the Customs, commanded by Capt. Amos, that she found it expedient, to save the rest of her lading, to throw 200 tubs of spirits over board, which were afterwards picked up by Capt. Amos, and lodged in the Custom House at Shoreham.

## October 29ᵀᴴ 1798

A Revenue Cutter lately chased another in the service of the smugglers so closely off Bletchington, that the latter, the better to effect her escape, was compelled to throw a great part of her cargo overboard, which was no sooner made known to the soldiers in barracks there, than they took to the water like spaniels, and saved between two and three hundred tubs of geneva, without any accident attending them. A Custom-house officer soon after appeared at the barracks, in hopes of being admitted to a share of the prize, but the soldiers disputing his title. he thought it prudent to relinquish his claim, and depart without his anticipated booty.

## April 28<sup>TH</sup> 1800

On Tuesday morning Mr. Whitpain, Officer of the Customs assisted by a party of Light Dragoons, seized on the beach near Broadwater. between three and four hundred casks and bags. containing brandy, rum, and tobacco, which the smugglers had just landed. but by the activity of the above officer were prevented from conveying away. The goods were afterwards safely lodged in his Majesty's warehouse at Shoreham.

# THEFT

## 7<sup>TH</sup> January 1788

The following singular circumstances attended the Lewes coach on its way from London, a few days since: After the carriage had got some miles out of town, the outside passengers conceived they heard a kind of groaning in the boot, and mentioned the same to the coach-man, who, supposing the noise to proceed from their own imaginations, and not from any real cause, disregarded it and drove on; but the same noise, being some little time afterwards heard again, he stopt the coach, and for the satisfaction of his passengers, unloaded the boot, where, however, he found nothing to account for the strange notion (as he thought) they had entertained and, mounting his box, drove on to Godstone, where he stopped to break-fast and change horses afterwards proceeded on his journey without further interruption till he got within a few miles of East Grinstead, where the like noise being again repeated, one of the passengers said he was sure the coach must be possessed of with something it ought not to be and swore that he would not go a step further with it unless 'twere first thoroughly examined, whereupon, the coachman proceeded to unload the boot entirely, and having got every article

*Horsham Gaol*

out except a large box, weighing near three quarters of a ton, to his very great astonishment discovered peeping through the straw at the bottom something like a human head, and on removing the said box found lying on his back thereunder a little ragged boy, who, on being taken out, appeared to be not more than five years old; being asked how he came there, answered, he had got into the thing (meaning the boot) the overnight to sleep and begged they would not hurt him. The passengers believed his story and made a collection for him, and the coach going up conveyed him back to London. What appears most extraordinary is that the child should lie so quiet during the whole time the coach was loading, and when such a quantity of heavy luggage was thrown promiscuously upon him, the boot being quite full; again, while the coach stopped at Godstone, where he was not heard even to breathe nor any time to groan, but, of necessity, when by the shakings and squattings of the coach the luggage pressed painfully upon him, and after all, to have received not the least hurt! 'Tis not impossible, but he may belong to a set of scheming depredators who might have had a design on the coach.

## 17TH August 1789

About 2 o'clock on Friday morning last, the house of Mrs. Shelley, Lewes, was burglariously broken into and robbed of diverse articles of plate, amounting in value to upwards of fifty pounds. The next morning two Jews, who travelled the country with pens, sealing wax and slippers, and who lodged the preceding night at a public house, near to that in which the robbery was committed, were taken up at Brighthelmston, on suspicion of being concerned with the burglary; and they now stand committed to the house of correction at Lewes, for further examinations, having given a bad account of themselves.

The same afternoon another man with stolen plate found upon him was apprehended, by John Hawcock on East Grinstead Common, and afterwards examined by Thomas Wally Partington Esq., who fully committed him to Horsham gaol to take his trial for the offence. He was not long before seen in company with three other men and a woman who unluckily escaped. The prisoner was committed by the name of Thomas Smith.

### September 7TH 1789
In the dead of night on Tuesday last, the house of John Taylor, of Erridge Green, in the parish of Frant, was broken into by two villains, who after binding the poor old man and his wife together in their bed with a cord they had provided for that purpose from a neighbouring barn, robbed two guineas, 10 shillings, two half crowns and one 5 shilling piece, in silver, a hat and two buckles, and a knife and then made off with their booty, leaving the aged pair to liberate themselves, which they at last effected by mumbling with their bandage, with their gums, for as to teeth they had few or none. The robbers threatened the lives of this defenceless couple with a scoring axe, till they had obtained information where they kept their money, which was in a chest in the same room, and which they immediately rifled.

### September 21ST 1789
Last Wednesday morning, the house of a farmer, at Wadhurst, while the family were employed in the harvest field, was broke into, and robbed of cash to the amount of £330, which he had a few days before collected for the purpose of placing it out at interest. A man named Stevens is taken up on suspicion of the robbery, and from

circumstance there is but too great reason to believe him guilty. None of the money was found upon him; but something had been observed to hang very heavy in his coat before he was apprehended, when he had no coat on, so that it is thought he had concealed both money and coat together. The money was in a day or two to have been deposited with Mr. Stove, Attorney-at-Law, Mayfield

## August 1ˢᵀ 1791

Early on Thursday morning a man was shot at, and considerably wounded in the garden of Mr. Hearndon, at the West Sheaf, in Malling Street, Lewes, where he had gotten for the purpose of robbing it. He made of unknown, but in his escape dropped a large quantity of blood.

## April 7ᵀᴴ 1794

At our late assizes at East Grinstead the following circumstances occurred which tends to prove how little the dread of justice operates in the minds of those whom daily practice has hardened in their offences. On the first day in the evening, as the Crown Jury was going into court to try the prisoners, two of them had their pockets picked, one of four and the other of five guineas, which they soon after discovered, and proclaimed aloud in Court, as a caution to others! and to put them on their guard against the dexterity of those nimble fingered depredators, when it appeared that they had not commenced their practice on the Jurors, but on some other persons, one of whom had lost nine guineas, and his fellow sufferers their watches. We hear that every Assizes on the home circuit was honoured with the attendance of the above pickpockets, and 'tis said that they obtained more fees by the agility of their fingers than all the Counsel did together by the flippancy of their tongues.

## August 17ᵀᴴ 1795

Whereas it has been the custom for post boys on their return home, to take up passengers and retain the hire for their own use, to the great loss of the post masters, and very great injury of their chaises and horses. We, whose names are hereunder set, do acquaint the public, that anyone riding in our returning chaises in future, must expect to pay the full hire; and we likewise offer a reward of half a guinea to anyone that will give information of any of our postboys taking up passengers on their return without our consent, or accounting to us for the full hire; and our postboys are to take notice that the first offender will be immediately discharged.

Witnesseth our hands this 15th day of August 1795. John Hich, Thomas Tilt, Scott and Owden, John Baulcomb, W. Henwood (Brightelmston), Robert Dunn, James Piddington, Richard Goddard (Lewes).

N.B.—Any postmaster may have his name added to this advertisement by sending it to the Printer postage paid.

### 26TH September 1796

On Tuesday a labourer at Horsham Barracks having been taken suddenly ill, a subscription of halfpence was set on foot by the other workmen for his support, one of whom having discovered that he had through mistake given a guinea with his copper contribution, went and demanded it of the person employed in the collection. The collector positively denied having received it, and on a search being demanded declared he would by no means submit to such a degradation; on force being resorted to, he resolutely knocked down three men who first laid hands upon him, but was at length over-powered, and the guinea found concealed on his person; in consequence of which he was mounted on a piece of timber and carried amid the hoots and hisses of his companions along the barrack ground and through the town; and was afterwards ignominiously dismissed from his employment.

### March 27TH 1797

A box containing four gold watches, valued at between eighty and ninety pound, was lately stolen from one of the Chichester Stage Coaches, by a young man who acted in the capacity of boot-catcher, an Inn, in that City, as appeared afterwards his own confession, when taken into custody on suspicion of the robbery. Three of the watches have been since traced out and recovered, but the fourth, purchased at second-hand by a travelling Jew, who cannot be found, is still missing. One was left in pledge for a guinea with a waiter in this town [Lewes], who on being applied to instantly surrendered it, and in proof of his want of knowledge to discover its value, said that he rejected the proffered purchase at three guineas. The one of which the Jew got possession was disposed of by the robber, at Blatchington Barracks.

## 27TH March 1797

Since a reward of ten guineas has been advertised for the apprehension of the three sheep-stealers who absconded from Steyning and Beeding, six or seven others of the gang have also fled. The whole gang, it now appears, consists of 16 or 17.

## 10TH April 1797

On Friday Morning, a soldier went into the shop of Mr. Pain, butcher in this town [Lewes] and stole therein four ribs of fine beef, with which he was seen to march off deliberately as if he had bought and paid for it; indeed the person who saw him in the act of carrying it away supposed he had done so.

## June 5TH 1797

On Saturday last, John Steward, of the Royal Artillery, was, by T Harben and R Stone Esqs., committed to the prison at Seaford for burglariously entering the dwelling house of Mrs Washer, of that place, the night before, and feloniously stealing therein ten women's shifts, ten pair of cotton stocking, six pocket handkerchiefs and three bottles of brandy.

## June 26TH 1797

Potter, who at the last Quarter Sessions for Seaford, received sentence of transportation, and the Artilleryman confined with him in the prison of that place, for a burglary in the house of Mrs Washer, were discovered a few days since in an attempt to make their escape. The Corporation having but one set of fetters, they, on the Artilleryman's committal, were taken off Potter and put upon him;

these irons they had contrived to saw off, after which they proceeded to make a breach in the ceiling of the prison, in order to get into the Town Hall (which is over it), and from thence into the street; and it is thought they would have effected their purpose, had they remained undiscovered an hour longer, An order, we understand, has since been received for removing the Artilleryman to a place of greater security, at one of the neighbouring forts.

## July 17TH 1797

At the Quarter Sessions at Seaford on Thursday last, John Steward, tried for burglariously and feloniously breaking into the dwelling house of Mrs. Washer and stealing therein sundry articles of wearing apparel, was convicted of the felony and sentenced to seven years transportation.

John Watford, convicted on the evidence of his nephew, Charles Watford, an accomplice, of stealing six fowls, the property of Mr. Blaker, of Portslade, was sentenced to fourteen years transportation. James Watford and William Hallet, tried for stealing eighteen fowls, the property of Mr. Hansome of Albourne; and Thomas Wright for stealing several fowls and a woollen great coat, in an outhouse of Mr. Ellman of Glynde, were severally convicted on the evidence of said Charles Watford, an accomplice, and brother to James, and each of them sentenced to seven years transportation.

Matthew Shepstone concerned in the the robbery at Albourne, was ordered to be recommitted for a week and then to be publicly whipped at the cart's tail and discharged

Note: This was the heaviest Sessions we ever remember to have witnessed here [Lewes]; the business of which gave novelty to the Records of the Court, and we believe there had been no former instance of four persons being sentenced to transportation, nor of the terms being, in any case where a similar punishment had been inflicted, extended to fourteen years.

## 6TH November 1797

About nine o'clock on Saturday evening, a man was seen to take a large piece of pickled pork from the stall of Mr. Paine, butcher in this town (Lewes) and after a short chase, taken. He dropt the pork, weighing about 19lbs, in his flight.

## November 13TH 1797
A little after twelve o'clock on Saturday night, some persons who had the appearance of gentlemen fond of FUN, were observed amusing themselves with the brass rappers affixed to the front doors of many houses in this town [Lewes] and the effect of their amusement was the next morning made visible by the invisibility of three rappers and a half. Several others were found in a situation which proved that their strength had resisted the violence of their assailants.

## November 21ST 1797
The Knights of the Knockers were again very busy here on Saturday night last and the many RAPPERLESS doors which appeared the next morning evidenced the dexterity of those nocturnal depredators.

## November 27TH 1797
Early on Monday morning last the pantry attached to the Earl of Egremont's Mansion House at Petworth was broken into and robbed of two silver soup ladles, some table spoons and a quantity of edibles by some villains, who got clear off with their booty; but for the apprehension and conviction of whom his Lordship offers a reward of one hundred pounds.

## January 8TH 1798
One night last week the Turnpike Toll-House at Ashcombe, near this town (Lewes) was broke open and robbed of several trifling articles. And a few nights preceding, the hen roost of John Boys, Esq., of Ashcombe was completely untiled, 'tis supposed for the purpose of getting at the poultry; but the robbers having been disturbed, and Mr. Boys having ever since employed a servant to guard his premises, the thieves have been disappointed of their chickens from that quarter.

Numberless other depredations were last week committed on

hen-roosts in this neighbourhood, and we are sorry to say, with better success than at Ashcombe.

## January 15TH 1798

GEESE STOLEN. Whereas on the night of the 4th inst. three Geese were stolen from the premises of Mr. Hickes, at Laughton, in the County of Sussex— A reward of FIVE GUINEAS will be paid by Mr. Hickes, to any person or persons giving information of the offender or offenders, so that he or they may be convicted, over and above a reward of TWO GUINEAS to be paid by Mr. Attree, Attorney, Treasurer to the Laughton Society for prosecuting Thieves, on conviction of offenders.   January 12, 1798.

## July 2ND 1798

A gentleman in this neighbourhood [Lewes] who a few weeks ago lost a letter case containing bank-notes to the amount of Forty Pounds, and a few worthless memorandums, had last week the satisfaction of knowing his book had been picked up, by the receipt of a billet, enclosing all the memorandums, except those signed by the bankers, which the honest finder had on some account or other omitted to put with the rest. The letter, which was put in a Penny-Post Office in London, is as follows:

"Sir. I happened to pick up a pocket book as I rode along the King's high-road and on examining it take this opportunity of sending back those papers inclosed which by so doing I hope serves you."

## September 3RD 1798

On last Monday evening as the Rev. Doctor Green of Steyning. was returning home from Wiston, he was overtaken by a soldier who asked him his way to Steyning. when the Doctor answered that he was going there, and if he chose he might accompany him, but they had not walked far together before the soldier drew his bayonet, and demanded the Doctor's watch and money. which he gave him, luckily not having more than ten shillings in his pockets. The robber on observing the watch to be an old one and apparently not of much value, returned it, and made off with the cash. The Doctor on arriving at Steyning, learned that not long before there had been at a public house a soldier answering the description of the one that had robbed him who said he belonged to the Sussex Militia stationed at Dover, and that Captain Poyntz had sent him from there to Cowdray for a dog. Several persons went in pursuit of him, but without effect.

### September 10<sup>TH</sup> 1798

The footpad who robbed the Rev. Doctor Green, near Steyning, as mentioned in our last, it can hardly be doubted, was the soldier who had but a short time before quitted a public-house at the above place. he being, as it has since appeared, a deserter from the Sussex Militia. and having been tried for a similar offence at one of our late Assizes. but of which he was acquitted.

### January 14<sup>TH</sup> 1799

On the night of the 11th of January instant, William Martin Cordwainer eloped from the House of James Chambers, at the sign of the Red Lion, on Ashington Common, and is strongly suspected of having stolen from the apartment where he slept, a man's hat and great coat; and from the shop where he worked, one pair of mens new Half-Boot-Shoes, one pair of low shoes. one pair of old shoes— new soled and heeled—two four ounce Bottoms of Flax Thread, one leather apron and wallet.

The said Wm. Martin is slender made, about 5 feet 3 or 4 inches high, rather round shouldered, lightish complexion, the forepart of his head bald; he said he was about 43 years of age; he is marked on his left arm with the letters W.M. and an anchor; and said he belonged to the town of Hastings. where he served his apprenticeship. He lately worked for a short time with Mr. Bailey? at Steyning. A reward of One Guinea is hereby offered by the said James Chambers, for the apprehending of the said Wm. Martin; and the further sum of Two Guineas by the Ashington Society for prosecuting thieves. etc. on his being convicted of stealing any of the above mentioned articles.

## June 3ʳᵈ 1799

Whereas on Sunday, the 26th ult., it was discovered that the Parish Church of Henfield had, by force and violence, been feloniously entered st the vestry window, by some person or persons, who, after breaking open two chests, which contained nothing of value, stole a Bottle of Tent Wine, and made off. A reward of TWENTY GUINEAS is therefore, hereby offered, for the apprehension of the offender or offenders, to be paid on the conviction of him or them, by the churchwardens of the said parish of Henfield.

## June 10ᵀᴴ 1799

On Monday last, a man calling himself William Neale, was apprehended in a field in the parish of Worth, in this county, on suspicion of felony, having in his possession, a short-handled fry pan, two pit saws, a linen bag containing 7 loaves of bread, another linen bag containing a number of dried herrings, part of a sack marked "J.M. Rotherfield, J.M. Crowborough" and divers other articles. Neale had lately been conveyed by a vagrant's pass from Kingstone(!) in Surrey, to Chailey near this town which he says is the place of his settlement. On being taken before a magistrate. Mr. Tredcroft, of Horsham, he gave a very unsatisfactory account of the manner of becoming possessed of the articles found on him: first saying he received them from Mr. Cole of Godstone, and afterwards of his Mother who lived near Felbridge.

## July 15ᵀᴴ 1799

Thomas Pettit, alias Jigg, the noted horse-stealer of Jevington, in this county, was at the late Assizes for the county of Wilts, held at Salisbury, capitally convicted and received sentence of death.

## July 22ᴺᴰ 1799

We find that John is the real Christian name of Pettit, alias Jigg, the noted horse stealer of Jevington, whom we mentioned in our last to have been capitally convicted and sentenced to death at the late Salisbury Assizes and not Thomas, as lastly assumed by him. If passing under a variety of names is to be taken as a proof of the frequency of his predatory excursions it may be presumed (and indeed is not doubted) he has been very active in his vocation, having been committed by the names of, Thomas Wilson, alias Pettits, alias Jack Jigg, alias Gibbs, alias Jigg, alias Morgan, alias Williams!

A report is prevalent here [Lewes] that the above notorious Offender has again contrived to slip his neck out of the halter, but on what authority we are unable to say.

## January 6TH 1800

One night last week the house of W. Franklin, Esq,. at Muntham, in this county was broke into and robbed of money, bank-bills, and other valuables to a very considerable amount; but we hear, a box was the next day discovered in the garden, which contained the greatest part of the stolen property.

## January 20TH 1800

Whereas Wm. Brown, of Washington, in the county of Sussex, Labourer, stands charged with feloniously stealing A EWE SHEEP, the property of Mr. Jeffery, of Washington aforesaid for which he has absconded.

A Reward of FIVE GUINEAS is therefore hereby offered for the apprehending of the said Wm. Brown, to be paid on his conviction, by the Treasurer of the Washington Society for prosecuting thieves, etc.

The said Wm. Brown is a short squat man, dark complexion, black straight hair, about 23 years of age; has a powder mark on his arm, and is supposed to have deserted from His Majesty's Navy about two years since.

## May 19TH 1800

Whereas on Friday night, May 16, or early on Saturday morning, The warehouse belonging to Mr. Philip Turner, of Easthoathly, was broken open and robbed of one large Cheshire Cheese, four or five Derby ditto, and one side and a half of dried bacon. Any person giving information of the offender or offenders, so that he or they may be apprehended and convicted. shall receive a reward of TWENTY POUNDS, to be paid by me. PHILIP TURNER, Easthoathly.

## INDEX OF SURNAMES

# INDEX OF PLACE-NAMES

79